Old Los Angeles

**BY KIM COOPER
WITH DICK BLACKBURN**

Published in 2016 by Herb Lester Associates Ltd

How To Find Old Los Angeles
Text © Kim Cooper
Additional text by Dick Blackburn © Herb Lester Associates Ltd 2016
Cover illustration by Dustin Wallace © Herb Lester Associates Ltd 2016

Herb Lester Associates has asserted its right to be identified as the author of this Work in accordance with the Copyright, Design & Patents Act 1988.

All rights reserved. No part of this publication may be reproduced, stored in a retrieval system, or transmitted in any form or by any means, electronic, mechanical, photocopying, recording or otherwise, without the prior permission of the copyright holder.

A CIP catalogue record for this book is available from the British Library

ISBN: 978-1-910023-67-9

Printed and bound in the United Kingdom by The Westdale Press Ltd
Cover: Cocoon offset 100% recycled board
Pages: Cocoon offset 100% recycled paper

Herb Lester Associates Ltd are committed to printing and publishing in the United Kingdom using 100% recycled materials wherever possible.

Herb Lester Associates Limited Reg. No 7183338

To see the full range of Herb Lester books, guides and products
visit herblester.com

Table of Contents

1. Downtown / Chinatown / Lincoln Heights 7

2. East Los Angeles / Boyle Heights 19

3. Echo Park / Silver Lake / Los Feliz / Highland Park 21

4. Glendale / Pasadena / South Pasadena / Eagle Rock 29

5. Hollywood 35

6. Mid-City 45

7. San Fernando Valley 53

8. San Gabriel Valley 57

9. South Bay 67

10. South Los Angeles County 71

11. West Hollywood 77

12. Westside and beaches 79

Index 91

Canters
FAIRFAX
RESTAURANT
OPEN 24 HO
BAKE
OPEN ALL N

LOS ANGELES, ITS CRITICS SAY, HAS NO MORE RESPECT FOR ITS PAST THAN FOR AN EMPTY PAPER CUP. LIKE MOST DIGS AIMED AT THE BIG ORANGE, THIS SIMPLY ISN'T TRUE.

A young metropolis, just a few generations removed from the tectonic shift from Spanish land grants to American statehood, Los Angeles boasts one of the nation's first and strongest historic preservation ordinances, courtesy of enlightened city planner Calvin Hamilton. All across its 503 square miles and 88 municipalities, you can find thriving historic establishments, dishing out chili dogs and cheesecakes, sidecars and self-realisation, all with a heaping side of Southern California soul.

This book is intended as a pocket guide to worthy pockets of old Los Angeles commerce and culture, from La Puente to La Cienega, Pacific Coast Highway to Hollywood Boulevard. It includes bakeries, bars, bookshops, bowling alleys and many fine things that don't begin with the letter B. Some of these sites are featured on my Esotouric bus tours; others are personal favourites. Each one is a stamp in the informal passport of the true Angeleno.

It is my hope that this book inspires many happy hours of exploration in this magnificent, misunderstood city that hides its charms from cynics, but rewards the earnest seeker with riches unimaginable.

Kim Cooper
Los Angeles, August 2016

Downtown / Chinatown Lincoln Heights

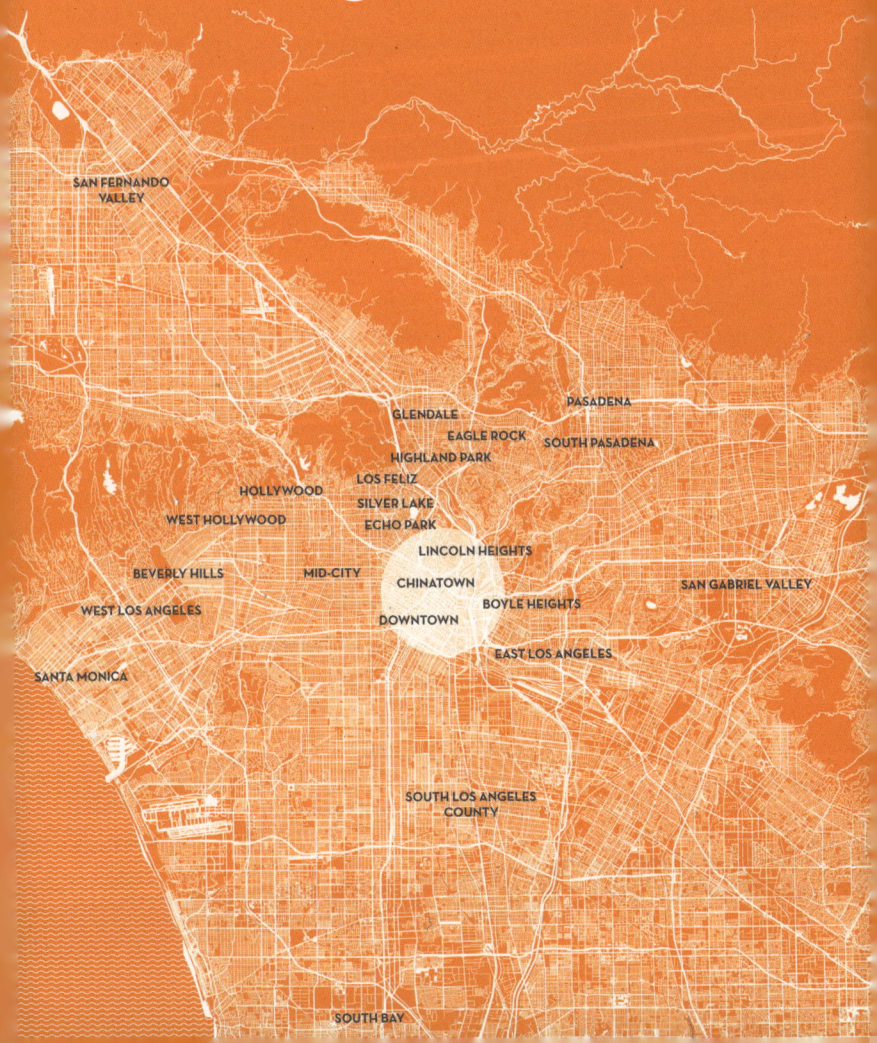

DOWNTOWN / CHINATOWN / LINCOLN HEIGHTS

ANGELS FLIGHT RAILWAY

In the 1880s the burghers of Los Angeles erected magnificent Victorian mansions on Bunker Hill, a craggy promontory from which they could gaze out over the young city, from riverside vineyards to the sea. But soon, the mansions were boarding houses, then red-tagged as slum housing. By 1970, Bunker Hill was leveled, its old world charms unfit for the modern world. But Angels Flight — Colonel Eddy's wonderful orange and black funicular railway that connected the hill dwellers with the ordinary world — survived. The redevelopment agency promised, and in 1996 it returned the wee enclosed escalator to service. Its second life has been troubled, with one death and two lengthy service outages. But the gorgeous station house still stands, and cars Olivet and Sinai are ready for service. They are the last survivors of lost Bunker Hill.

351 S Hill St., 90013 / Tel: 213 626 1901

BILTMORE HOTEL

When the Renaissance Revival Biltmore Hotel (Schultze and Weaver, 1922) opened facing John Parkinson's magnificent Pershing Square park (1910), it was the largest and most elegant hostelry on the West Coast. And while Pershing Square has been remuddled into a postmodern day-glo concrete disaster, the beautiful Biltmore has hardly changed at all. A crackerjack staff stalks the halls, touching up details on Giovanni Smeraldi's murals and sculptures with tiny brushes. In the long bar off the Galleria Real (the hotel's central hall), you'll find modern mixologists crafting classic cocktails, live jazz and a lovely room with corbelled ceiling, fluted columns and flattering lighting. It's popular with the after work crowd and hotel celebrants.

506 S Grand Ave., 90071 / Tel: 213 612 1011
Daily: 4pm-2am

BRADBURY BUILDING

From the 1950 film noir D.O.A., on up to Blade Runner — the downtown 1893 Bradbury Building has been used in countless films. Its five-storied courtyard is brightly illuminated by natural light through a domed roof, encircled by wrought-iron staircases, Mexican-tile floors, Belgian-marble stairs, cage elevators and ornamental cast-iron railings. It continues to be both a tourist attraction and a working office building.

304 South Broadway, 90013 / Tel: 213 626 1893

BROADWAY THEATER DISTRICT

Plenty of urban downtowns have hip hotels and restaurants, but only Los Angeles can boast the nation's largest National Register Historic Theater District, with a dozen vintage performance houses. Here in the movie capital there was room for 15,000 people to see shows simultaneously, from

Bradbury Building

DOWNTOWN / CHINATOWN / LINCOLN HEIGHTS

the wee Cameo nickelodeon (1910) to the magnificently equipped Los Angeles (1931). Today, not a single theater regularly shows movies. Most are vacant, used for storage or occasional filming. The restored Orpheum (1926) and United Artists (1927) are concert venues and the State (1921) is a church. Interior tours are sometimes offered by the Los Angeles Conservancy and Los Angeles Historic Theatre Foundation. To stroll down Broadway is to pass through the history of popular entertainment, and the increasingly elaborate temples built to house it.

CARAVAN BOOK STORE

Second generation bookman Leonard Bernstein's one-room Caravan is the last remnant of a once-thriving Bookseller's Row centred around the main library. The sign in the window promises "Avant Garde, First Editions, Poetry" and you'll find all that, plus Californiana, Civil War History, Fine Bindings, Cookery, Vintage Prints and Postcards. But what's really on offer is a traditional bookshop experience of the type that's too rare: a chance to make yourself at home among frequently updated stock while savouring the incomparable perfume of old ink and wood pulp. You won't be bothered while browsing, but if you want a recommendation or to know more about the lost world of L.A. bookshops, the lavishly mustachioed proprietor at the back desk is happy to oblige.

550 S Grand Ave., 90071 / Tel: 213 626 9944
Mon-Fri: 11.30am-6pm; Sat: 12noon-5pm

CICADA CLUB RESTAURANT

A swanky men's clothing store from 1928, this sumptuous downtown time capsule's richly appointed wood wall panels, columns and Lalique glass now house a pricey-but-good restaurant, and bar up on the mezzanine. Often hired out for private parties and film shoots, it is also the setting for Sunday evening specials, each featuring a 1920s or 1930s-styled dance band or orchestra accompanying dinner.

617 South Olive St., 90014 / Tel: 213 488 9488
Thu-Sat: 5.30pm-9pm; Sun: 6pm-11pm

CLIFTON'S CAFETERIA

Clifford Clinton was a visionary who designed immersive proto-Disneyland environments 20 years before Walt's theme park, fed the hungry, had his home bombed by cops while bringing down a corrupt Mayor and ran a terrific chain of home-style cafeterias. Clifton's Brookdale, at the historic terminus of Route 66, was the last family-run outpost, sold and shuttered in 2010. New owner Andrew Meieran did considerable restoration, changing the focus from home cooking to fancy drinking and adding a giant faux redwood tree for aerialist acts. The woodsy first floor and mezzanine remain much as Clinton intended.

648 S Broadway, 90014 / Tel: 213 627 1673
Tue-Wed: 11am-10pm; Thu-Fri: 11am-2am;
Sat: 10am-2am; Sun: 10am-10pm

DOWNTOWN / CHINATOWN / LINCOLN HEIGHTS

COLE'S

Serving from the same space in the former Pacific Electric Car building since 1908, and now completely restored with stained glass, red-flocked wallpaper, full-length bar, booths, tables, and old signs and photos on the walls. This atmospheric bar is in competition with Philippe's, as the self-proclaimed inventor of the famous French dipped beef sandwich — a hot beef sandwich served with a beef dipping sauce. The hidden speakeasy deep within the restaurant is a recent addition, much loved by the craft cocktail crowd.

118 East 6th St., 90014 / Tel: 213 622 4090
Restaurant: Sun-Wed: 11am-10pm;
Thu: 11am-11pm; Fri-Sat: 11am-1am
Bar: Sun-Wed: 11.30am-12midnight;
Thu-Sat: 11am-2am

CONFLUENCE OF THE L.A. RIVER AND ARROYO SECO

There are prettier spots along the River, among them the nearby natural bottomed Glendale Narrows with islands dense with mature trees and bird life. But for pure old Los Angeles significance, the Confluence takes the prize. Here the waterways of the Arroyo Seco and Los Angeles River met, inspiring early settlers to build their town close enough to run an irrigation ditch, yet far enough to avoid seasonal flooding. Later, train hopping hobos made camp and left inscriptions that still survive. The original riverbed was channelised by the Army Corps of Engineers after the deadly 1938 flood. Today the Confluence is a vast, sometimes wet, concrete plane spanned by bridges. It can be accessed from a ramp off Avenue 19, just east of Figueroa. It's at once a beautiful industrial landscape and a reminder of a much sleepier Los Angeles.

EASTSIDE MARKET & ITALIAN DELI

Back when Chinatown was still Little Italy (1929), Joe Campagna and Domenic Pontrelli opened their hillside Eastside Market, supplying imported kitchen staples. In 1974, Johnny and Frank Angiuli, brothers who were longtime employees, purchased the market and added a deli counter. Word soon spread among the City Hall office crowd and Dodgers tailgaters that this was something special, and the market became an afterthought. If you like your sandwiches massive and piled high with every kind of meat in the case, the "D.A. Special" is it: sausage, meatball, pastrami and roast beef on a crusty bun. Regulars ask for the marinara sauce on the side, and dip.

1013 Alpine St., 90012 / Tel: 213 250 2464
Mon-Fri: 8am-4pm; Sat: 9am-3pm

GRAND CENTRAL MARKET

From 1917 through the early 2000s, the busy and beloved 30,000 square foot Grand Central Market offered a wide selection of cheap ethnic provisions and kitchen staples: snout-to-tail butchers and fishmongers, spice counters, bakeries, fruit and veg vendors, booze and sweets. Scattered among the grocers were a small number of prepared food stands. A recent reimagining has flipped the format, and now most vendors offer Instagrammable meals, at a higher price point. But the vast hall that spans a double lot between Broadway and Hill Streets retains its funky, democratic charm and provides some of the city's best people watching.

317 S Broadway, 90013 / Tel: 213 624 2378
Sun-Wed: 8am-6pm; Thu-Sat: 8am-10pm

HOP LOUIE

When the construction of Union Station took out L.A.'s historic Chinatown (and, not incidentally, the notorious red light district), the Chinese community was compensated with the development of a moderne, neon-drenched commercial centre a few blocks northwest. The five-tiered Golden Pagoda (1941) that now houses this bar and restaurant stands sentry as New Chinatown's tallest landmark. Nobody goes to New Chinatown for Chinese food anymore, and that goes double for Hop Louie. But the dimly-lit ground floor dive bar is a gem, full of local characters slurping the signature Scorpion Bowl cocktail, a rum, brandy, fruit juice and champagne concoction that you underestimate at your peril.

950 Mei Ling Way, 90012 / Tel: 213 628 4244
Restaurant: Mon-Fri: 11am-3pm & 5pm-9pm;
Sat-Sun: 11am-9pm; Bar, Daily: 4pm-2am

LA GOLONDRINA MEXICAN CAFÉ

When visiting Olvera Street, a more than slightly artificial theme park of pre-Anglo life in Los Angeles, look for the authentically old school La Golondrina. In 1930, popular restaurateur Consuelo Castillo de Bonzo, whose Spring Street establishment faced demolition, pulled in some political favours to get in on the ground floor of Christine Sterling's commercial development. The lively establishment has always featured live music and dancing, strong drinks and rich, cheesy fare. It's located in the Pelanconi House, an old winery that's the city's oldest firebrick building (1857). Snag a seat on the patio and watch the world go by.

17 Olvera St., 90012 / Tel: 213 628 4349
Mon: 10am-3pm; Tue-Thu: 10am-8pm;
Fri-Sat: 10am-9pm; Sun: 9.30am-8pm

LANZA BROTHERS MARKET

It looks like an ordinary corner market and liquor store in any industrial neighbourhood. But tucked inside is a counter-service sandwich joint, catering to passing truckers, downtown workers and residents of the adjacent Brewery Arts Complex. A rare survivor (since 1926) of Lincoln Heights' dispersed Italian-American community, Lanza Brothers scratches the lunch time itch with tall, paper-wrapped deli sandwiches packed with generously-cut Boar's Head brand

Broadway Theater District

DOWNTOWN / CHINATOWN / LINCOLN HEIGHTS

meats and cheeses, pickled peppers on the side, avocado on request. There are a few tables outside, but no atmosphere. A good picnic option en route to Dodger Stadium.

1803 N Main St., 90031 / Tel: 323 225 8977
Mon-Fri: 8am-8pm; Sat: 8.30am-6pm

LOS ANGELES CITY HALL

The platonic ideal of a modern City Hall, the gleaming white tower with its stepped ziggurat topper has been featured in countless films. Long the tallest building in the city — the building code banned construction that might eclipse it — City Hall remains a time capsule of boomtown 1926 construction. Post 9/11 security means you can't just walk up the monumental Spring Street steps and go exploring. Visitors with picture ID can enter through the metal detectors on the dingy Main Street side, then take a tiny elevator to the third floor. Admire the tile, metalwork and Zodiac ceiling, dense with symbolism. Take an express elevator to the 22nd floor and a local to the 26th. Steps lead up to the Observation Deck, with views over the city.

200 N Spring St., 90012 / Tel: 213 485 2121
Mon-Fri: 10am-5pm

LOS ANGELES PUBLIC LIBRARY

We almost lost LAPL's Central Branch to redevelopment in the 1980s; an arson fire gutted the stacks, but solidified support for the preservation of Bertram Grosvenor Goodhue's 1926 Art Deco temple of learning. It was here that Charles Bukowski, John Fante and Ray Bradbury educated themselves; Fante and Bradbury are honored with civic designations just outside. The library has expanded to the east, but the historic heart still beats. From Fifth Street, ascend by stair past the twin sphinx statues to the soaring atrium, decorated with Dean Cornwell's murals of the founding of California. Note the magnificent globe chandelier, each bulb representing a state in the union. The Children's Reading Room, formerly the Fiction Department beloved by Bukowski, has yet more charming California-themed murals and decorative concrete beams.

630 W 5th St., 90071 / Tel: 213 228 7000
Mon-Thu: 10am-8pm; Fri-Sat: 9.30am-5.30pm;
Sun: 1pm-5pm

LUMMIS HOUSE

Los Angeles has always attracted dreamers and visionaries, people drawn to all the possibilities of a culture of reinvention. Charles Fletcher Lummis was a Harvard kid with poetic ambitions who made himself famous sending out newspaper dispatches from his journey across the nation by foot. Along the way, he formed an abiding affection for the culture and architecture of the Southwest Indians and the unheralded history of pre-colonial America. Settling along the Arroyo, he built "El Alisal," a remarkable castle-like stone house inspired by the pueblos of New

Los Angeles City Hall

PHOENIX BAKERY
CHINATOWN
FAMOUS BIRTHDAY CAKES

雙鳳

DOWNTOWN / CHINATOWN / LINCOLN HEIGHTS

Mexico, but with many eclectic DIY details — look for the glass plate photo negatives embedded in window panes. Here, Lummis organised to save the California Missions, held court in the city's first great cultural salon and staged traditional Spanish fiestas where he recorded old songs and stories. The landmark house in its native garden is owned, and rather meagerly managed, by the city.

200 E AVENUE 43, 90031 / TEL: 818 243 6488
SAT-SUN: 10AM-3PM

ORIGINAL PANTRY CAFE

"We Never Close" states this downtown 1924 L.A. landmark. And they mean it — the owners claim to have no keys to the front door. Some of the waiters and waitresses seem to be as old as this never-restyled time-warp beanery; you wouldn't think it strange for Charlie Chaplin to run past its weathered booths and counter stools pursued by the Keystone Kops. Great sourdough bread and a relish bowl set you up, followed by filling, well-prepared comfort food at exceptional value. It's often crowded through the wee hours of the morning, with free parking across the street.

877 SOUTH FIGUEROA, 90017 / TEL: 213 972 9279
DAILY: 24 HOURS

PHILIPPE THE ORIGINAL

Uprooted from its 1920s location in the 1950s, to accommodate construction of the 101 Freeway, Philippe's today is just down the street from historic Chinatown. The old-time ambience is further enhanced by long communal tables, sawdust on the floors and a 10-cent cup of coffee. Jars of homemade mustard sauce are on sale at the register. Unable to say who was the first — Philippe's or Cole's — to invent the French Dip, we'll just say that both make excellent versions.

1001 NORTH ALAMEDA ST., 90012
TEL: 213 628 3781
DAILY: 6AM-10PM

PHOENIX BAKERY

When the city built New Chinatown to accommodate businesses evicted by construction of Union Station, the Chan family's Phoenix Bakery was one of the first to open. That was in 1938, a few blocks south of the current store (1977). Now under third generation ownership, the bakery offers traditional Chinese pastries like mooncakes, sesame lotus balls, almond cookies and honey-glazed fried butterfly twists. But nearly everyone who walks through the door is picking up "that" cake, the two-layer strawberry, cream, almond and sponge masterpiece invented by grandpa Lun Chan in the late 1940s. Not too sweet and packed with fruit, it's been the star of uncountable Los Angeles celebrations, and is available in single serving sizes too.

969 N BROADWAY, 90012 / TEL: 213 628 4642
DAILY: 9AM-7.30PM

HOW TO FIND OLD LOS ANGELES   17

DOWNTOWN / CHINATOWN / LINCOLN HEIGHTS

THE PLAZA

When the Franciscan padres needed a site for the secular village of El Pueblo de Nuestra Señora la Reina de los Ángeles del Río de Porciúncula (1781), they chose one near the river and the Chumash village of Yang-na. The 44 settlers, with much native assistance, laid out streets and a public plaza, built adobe homes, church and graveyard. From this point grew all of Los Angeles. With the decades, the neglected buildings around the Plaza were given over to vice. Enter Christine Sterling, who in 1926 sought to save the endangered Avila Adobe. Encouraged by her success, she set out to save all of Olvera St., a filthy alley that she transformed into a lively tourist attraction celebrating the Spanish Colonial era. While inauthentic, Olvera Street is old enough to itself be historic. Step into the restored Avila Adobe and feel the centuries slip away.

SAN ANTONIO WINERY

Early settlers planted grapes along the banks of the L.A. River, and by 1890, Los Angeles was the centre of the western wine industry. But development and legal problems pushed the vintners out, and today, just one downtown winery remains. Santo Cambianica founded San Antonio Winery in 1917, obtaining special permission to produce sacramental church wine during the dark days of prohibition. When booze began to flow again, non-Catholics could again enjoy their products. Although the grapes are now shipped in from Central and Northern California, wines are still produced down by the river by the fourth generation owners. The public is welcome to tour the landmarked facility, visit the tasting room and enjoy a cafeteria style meal.

737 Lamar St., 90031 / Tel: 323 223 1401
Sun-Thu: 9am-7pm; Fri-Sat: 9am-8pm

UNION STATION

The iron horse transformed a sleepy Spanish village into a booming Anglo metropolis, but by the mid-1920s something had to be done to contain the tangle of unrelated train tracks, stations and operators clogging the land between the river and downtown business district. The answer was Union Station (1939), a one-stop shop for passenger rail needs. To build it, old Chinatown's notorious red light district had to be seized and razed, with a cute modern Chinatown constructed to the west. In its place rose the last great American train station, a magnificent Art Deco / Mission Revival pile by John Parkinson. Beautifully restored and thrumming with energy, it is a functional transit hub, a cathedral of urbanity and where one goes to get a shoeshine from Marco Ramirez, one of our favourite Los Angeles characters.

800 N Alameda St., 90012
Daily: 24 hours

Boyle Heights
East Los Angeles

SAN FERNANDO VALLEY

GLENDALE
PASADENA
EAGLE ROCK
SOUTH PASADENA
HIGHLAND PARK
LOS FELIZ
HOLLYWOOD
SILVER LAKE
WEST HOLLYWOOD
ECHO PARK
LINCOLN HEIGHTS
BEVERLY HILLS
MID-CITY
CHINATOWN
BOYLE HEIGHTS
SAN GABRIEL VALLEY
WEST LOS ANGELES
DOWNTOWN
EAST LOS ANGELES
SANTA MONICA

SOUTH LOS ANGELES
– COUNTY

SOUTH BAY

BOYLE HEIGHTS / EAST LOS ANGELES

AL & BEA'S

Duck into this modest shack in the shadow of Hollenbeck Police Station, home of the ooey, gooey, careful-or-you'll-stain-your-shirt bean and cheese burrito, for a Mexican-American comfort food fix. Stock up on paper napkins and snag a spot on the tiny patio or dine al fresco in nearby Hollenbeck Park (1892), and find out why eastside folks have kept Al & Bea's dishing up the goods since 1966.

2025 E 1st St., 90033 / Tel: 323 267 8810
Mon-Sat: 9am-8pm; Sun: 9am-7pm

MANUEL'S ORIGINAL EL TEPEYAC CAFÉ

The appeal of this legendary eastside establishment is the monstruo burritos that can comfortably feed two to four adults. Mas grande is Manuel's Special weighing in at a whopping five pounds. Manuel constructed it supposedly to win a bet that he could make a burrito a customer could not finish. He won. It's a monster, and there's a good chance that anyone having a go at this will have enough left over to feed hungry people at home. The small interior, except for the Virgin Mary shrine, is strictly utilitarian: simple chairs around Formica-topped tables.

812 North Evergreen Ave., 90033 /
Tel: 323 268 1960 / 1961
Sun-Mon: 6am-9.45pm; Tue: 6am-8pm;
Wed-Thu: 6am-9.45pm; Fri- Sat: 6am-11pm

OTOMISAN

Although today a mostly Chicano neighbourhood, Boyle Heights was once the city's cultural melting pot. In this early suburb immigrants forgot their differences to embrace a new identity as Eastside Angelenos. Executive Order 9066, which caused Japanese-Americans to sell their businesses before being sent to internment camps in 1942, broke up the party. Though some families returned after the war, it was never the same. But one charming, family-run Japanese restaurant survives, with its vintage 1956 lunch counter and red vinyl booths, a time machine tribute to the Boyle Heights that was.

2506 E 1st St., 90033 / Tel: 323 526 1150
Mon-Sat: 11.30am-3pm & 4.30pm-9pm

PIONEER CHICKEN

A once-ubiquitous fast food chain founded in 1961 and immortalised in song by Warren Zevon as a nice place to score heroin. There are three surviving Pioneers in Los Angeles County, with this location physically nearest to the Echo Park original. The jaunty fat man driving a chuck wagon sign is a classic. Pioneer specialises in fried chicken that's extra crunchy on the outside, moist and tender on the inside. Old school sides include mashed potatoes, baked beans and corn on the cob.

904 S Soto St., 90023 / Tel: 323 262 4562
Daily: 10am-9.30pm

Echo Park / Silver Lake
Los Feliz / Highland Park

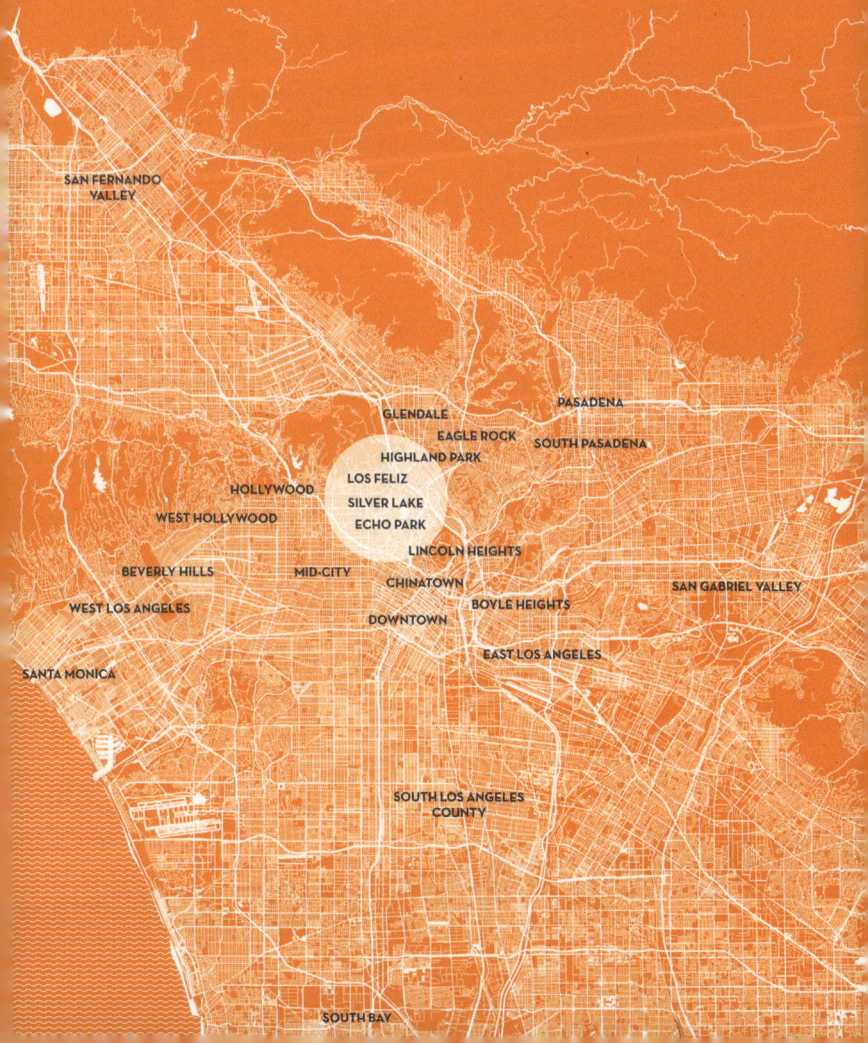

ECHO PARK / SILVER LAKE / LOS FELIZ / HIGHLAND PARK

ASTRO FAMILY RESTAURANT

Originally known as Donley's Coffee Shop, later Conrad's, and designed by master Googie architects Louis Armet and Eldon Davis in 1958, Astro makes a bold sculptural statement with its soaring white wing facade and green Swiss cheese steel support beams over the patio. Inside, the gleaming speckled black and white terrazzo floor reflects a neat line of plush counter stools. The fare is greasy spoon diner with a Greek twist, also with gentrified Silver Lake pricing, but it's a great spot for people watching, especially after the clubs let out.

2300 FLETCHER DRIVE, 90039 / TEL: 323 663 9241
DAILY: 24 HOURS

CARROLL AVENUE

Do you wish you could go back to Victorian Los Angeles? On the 1300 block of Carroll Avenue, in the early streetcar suburb of Angeleno Heights, you almost can. The National Register Historic District contains the city's finest collection of Victorian homes, most constructed around the boom year of 1888. After Bunker Hill was leveled in the 1960s, a preservationist fire began smouldering here in its sister neighbourhood. Residents restored homes, and endangered houses from other parts of town were moved onto vacant lots. With old street lights and buried electrical wires, the frequently filmed block has a wonderful way of making you forget the Hollywood freeway, just steps away.

DRESDEN ROOM

Pass on the food at this 1964 Los Feliz restaurant and call by after having dinner elsewhere for good drinks in the lounge (although beware, service can be iffy). Once ensconced in a leather booth, enjoy Marty and Elayne (Tuesday through Saturday nights) duet through their Sinatra-fied ring-a-ding thing amid the rock walls and gold metal pendant lamps. The two performers and The Dresden were featured in the 1990s indie movie hit Swingers.

1760 NORTH VERMONT AVE., 90027
TEL: 323 665 4294
MON-SAT: 4.30PM-2AM; SUN: 4.30PM-12MIDNIGHT

EL CID

Perched on a steep hill just west of Sunset Junction is the Spanish restaurant and nightclub that recently celebrated a half century of dinnertime flamenco shows. While 50 years is old for Los Angeles, the site has a richer story to tell. In the 1950s, it was the Cabaret Concert Theater, home to the wacky Billy Barnes Revue featuring game show legend Charles Nelson Reilly. In the 1920s, with a faux stone paint job, it was The Jail Cafe, where patrons banged cups on metal bars for service from waiters in striped pajamas and ate their chicken dinners without silverware. And in the teens, before the building was constructed, cinema pioneer D.W. Griffith filmed parts of Birth of A Nation on the hillside and adjacent

Carroll Avenue

ECHO PARK / SILVER LAKE / LOS FELIZ

cornfield. Today it sports a thriving weekend brunch trade, a flamenco-punctuated dinner service and occasional indie music shows.

4212 Sunset Boulevard, 90029
Tel: 323 668 0318
Mon-Fri: 6pm-2am; Sat: 3pm-2am;
Sun: 11am-12midnight

GRIFFITH PARK OBSERVATORY

In 1882 Colonel Griffith J. Griffith, having made a fortune in a gold-rush speculation, bought over 4,000 acres of Rancho Los Feliz. Fourteen years later he donated 3,000 acres as free parkland for the people of Los Angeles. Upon his death he willed funds for the construction of both the Observatory and Greek Theater within this, the largest municipal park in America. Broad hiking and horseback riding trails and narrow canyons wind up the hills to the Deco-domed Observatory best known for its appearance in Rebel Without A Cause. A bronze bust of James Dean stands nearby.

2800 East Observatory Road, 90027
Tel: 213 473 0800
Wed-Fri: 12noon-10pm; Sat-Sun: 10am-10pm

HERITAGE SQUARE

Los Angeles tore out the heart of its late 19th century Downtown residential district when Bunker Hill was demolished and flattened for redevelopment. One stubborn family had refused to negotiate to sell their beloved houses, and in 1969 the newly-landmarked Castle and Salt Box were moved five miles north to Montecito Heights, the seeds for a planned open-air museum of Los Angeles architecture. Tragically, both homes were soon destroyed by arsonists, but Heritage Square has grown into an unlikely city block of salvaged treasures in various states of restoration, including a rare octagonal house, several grand Victorian mansions, a church, a wee train station and a fully-stocked replica drugstore.

3800 Homer St., 90031 / Tel: 323 225 2700
Fri-Sun: 11.30am-4.30pm

Hollyhock House

HOLLYHOCK HOUSE

The only publicly owned and accessible Frank Lloyd Wright-designed home in Los Angeles, it also has the distinction of having never been lived in. The client was Aline Barnsdall, oil heiress, arts advocate and political gadfly, who was every bit as stubborn as Wright. The 1919-21 Mayan Revival-style project has house and gardens flowing together to showcase magnificent 360-degree city views. Barnsdall was unhappy with the final result, and gifted land and buildings to the city, which sold parcels off for a strip mall and hospital. Barnsdall had intended Olive Hill to be an arts colony; the city maintains a municipal gallery on site. The house itself recently reopened after a lengthy restoration.

4800 HOLLYWOOD BOULEVARD, 90027
TEL: 323 913 4030
THU-SUN: 11AM-3PM

HOUSE OF PIES

By some unlikely quirk, one restaurant in this defunct L.A.-based chain survives. Founded by International House of Pancakes creator Al Lapin, Jr.

HOW TO FIND OLD LOS ANGELES 25

Vista Theatre

and operated by franchise holders, the Los Feliz branch opened in 1969 and, according to a former manager, was a favourite of writer Charles Bukowski, who lived nearby. The corporation went belly up in the 1970s, leaving the franchise holders to sink or swim on their own. Most sank, but today the last House Of Pies standing still serves the community with simple diner fare, big booths, late night hours (closing when the bars do) and a giant selection of you know what.

1869 N VERMONT AVE., 90027
TEL: 323 666 9961
MON-FRI: 6.30AM-2AM; SAT-SUN: 7AM-2AM

JUDSON STUDIOS

English stained glass artisan William Lees Judson ran the USC College of Fine Arts on this site until 1910, at which time the building burned. The current structure, in the folk arts and crafts style, served the college through 1920, then became Judson's workshop. Today, David Judson, great-great-grandson of William, runs the business, restoring historic stained and leaded glass windows and crafting brand new ones. The public can attend occasional studio tours, or commission a piece to pass down to their own great-grandchildren.

200 S AVENUE 66, 90042
TEL: 800 445 8376 / 323 255 0131
TIMES VARY, CALL FOR DETAILS

HOW TO FIND OLD LOS ANGELES

RED LION TAVERN

Opened as a British pub (1959) by Ted Mandekic and Edward Pagliano, proprietors of French dip sandwich joint Cole's, the Red Lion took a turn to the east in 1963 with a German-style rebranding, and so it remains. The always busy Red Lion is three venues in one: the pub-like ground floor, the ratskeller-style middle bar, and a patio biergarten at the top of the stairs, all served by waitresses in traditional garb. There are plenty of German beers on tap, all the better to wash down giant plates of sausage and potato pancakes. And no, you're not seeing things: that is modernist master Richard Neutra's architecture office just across the street, from which he designed several notable homes in the surrounding Silver Lake hills.

2366 GLENDALE BOULEVARD, 90039
TEL: 323 662 5337
DAILY: 11AM–2AM

SISTER AIMEE'S PARSONAGE

In 1918, Aimee Semple McPherson rolled into town, a single mother with a gift for evangelising. She built a flock and then a grand tabernacle on Echo Park Lake, in which she staged "illustrated sermons" that were miniature Broadway musicals, each one starring blonde, smiling Aimee. Despite her remarkable Depression-era charitable work, a scandalous kidnap drama and unforgiving press would taint her reputation and obscure a fascinating life story. Get a glimpse at the real Sister Aimee with a visit to the gorgeous Spanish cottage where she lived and worked. Highlights include the Batchelder tile fireplace, cast-off braces abandoned by the miraculously healed and perhaps the city's loveliest tiled bathroom.

1801 PARK AVE., 90026 / TEL: 213 989 4444
MON-THU: 1PM–3PM; FRI: 10AM–1PM

TAIX

A rare vestige of L.A.'s once prominent French community, this restaurant (pronounced "Tex" and under fourth generation Taix family ownership) was founded in 1927, and fled the French district near Chinatown for Echo Park in 1962. With an eat-in bar, formal dining room and private banquet hall, the sprawling compound also plays host to occasional indie music and comedy events. The fare is bistro traditional — mussels, snails, frog legs, coq au vin — with soup served in tureens that the whole table can share. Pro tip: old school Angelenos still refer to the place as Les Freres Taix.

1911 W SUNSET BOULEVARD, 90026
TEL: 213 484 1265
MON-THU: 11.30AM–10PM; FRI: 11.30AM–11PM;
SAT: 12NOON–11PM; SUN: 12NOON–10PM

TAM O'SHANTER

Storied, Storybook style, Scots-themed restaurant (1922) was designed by Harry Oliver and founded by not-yet-legendary

ECHO PARK / SILVER LAKE / LOS FELIZ / HIGHLAND PARK

L.A. restaurateurs Lawrence Frank and Walter Van de Kamp (Van de Kamp's Bakeries, Lawry's The Prime Rib). The Disney animation studio was nearby, and Walt and his crew ate lunch here almost every day. (Walt's table is #31.) With its cosy, country tavern atmosphere, servers in fetching plaid ensembles and hidden nooks, the Tam has offered an escape from modern L.A. life for nearly a century. The menu is elevated comfort food. Save room for the legendary C.C. Brown's hot fudge sundae, the recipe straight from the (sadly defunct) Hollywood Boulevard establishment that invented the treat in 1906.

2980 LOS FELIZ BOULEVARD, 90039
TEL: 323 664 0228
DAILY: 11AM-12MIDNIGHT

TIKI-TI

With legendary Polynesian haunts such as The Islander, The Luau and Don The Beachcomber but a fading memory, fans of tikiana can rejoice that 92 authentic vintage tropical libations are being carefully concocted at this tiny Los Feliz boîte. In 1961, Ray Buhen, bartender at Beachcomber's back in 1937, opened his own 12-stool bar in this former violin shop. Today his son and grandson carry on his mixologist artistry amid netting, puffer fish and all manner of tiki souvenirs. As a final throwback, smoking is still permitted.

4427 WEST SUNSET BOULEVARD, 90027
TEL: 323 669 9381
WED-SAT: 4PM-2AM

TRAVEL TOWN

Tucked into a quiet section of Griffith Park is a nine-acre open air museum of the marvelous machines that brought people out to the growing metropolis of Los Angeles. Generations of Angelenoes got their first taste of rail travel as toddlers riding the roofless miniature train that circles the site. Grown ups will get a kick out of climbing on and in the vintage stationary locomotives, passenger cars and L.A. streetcars, including some dating back to the mid-19th century. Entry is free, with miniature train rides ticketed.

5200 ZOO DRIVE, 90027 / TEL: 323 662 5874
MON-FRI: 10AM-4PM; SAT-SUN: 10AM-5PM

VISTA THEATRE

Built on the site of D.W. Griffith's huge Babylon set for his 1916 silent masterpiece Intolerance, Bard's Hollywood Theater opened in 1923. While the exterior was done in Spanish Revival style, the interior was, like many other picture palaces in L.A. at the time — inspired by the discovery of King Tut's tomb — stunningly Egyptian. At this lovingly restored single-screen gem you won't see obscure art-house films or even those of old D.W., but its low prices, fine snack bar and more than generous legroom between rows, make viewing even standard Hollywood fare a lot more enjoyable than an overpriced Cineplex.

4473 SUNSET DRIVE, 90027 / TEL: 323 660 6639

Glendale / Pasadena
South Pasadena / Eagle Rock

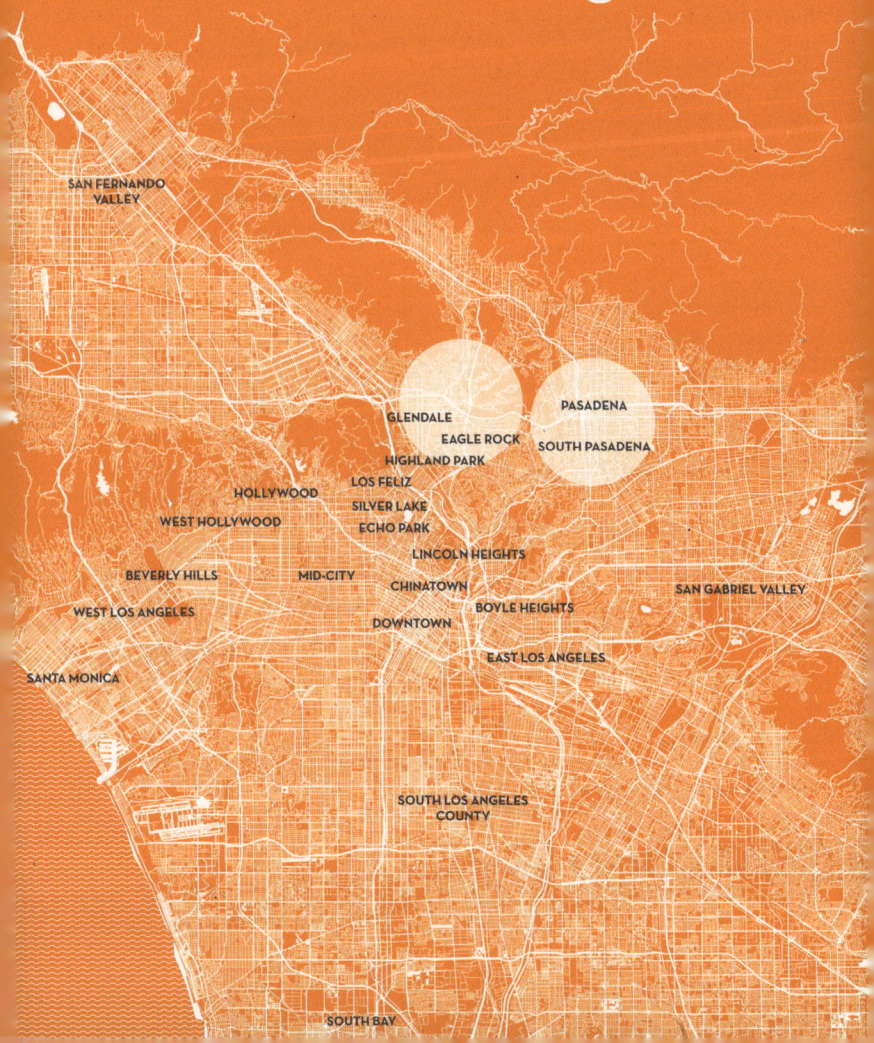

GLENDALE / EAGLE ROCK / PASADENA / SOUTH PASADENA

BRAND LIBRARY AND ART CENTER

While Southern California never had a true world's fair, we've got a replica of one of the grandest exotic pavilions from the great Chicago Fair of 1893 in the hills of Glendale. Developer Leslie C. Brand's mansion El Miradero (1904) is a gleaming white temple studded with minarets and stepped arches, beautifully situated above the town. Brand's widow Mary Louise willed the property to Glendale with the provision that it be used as a library and park. A modern extension hosts cultural lectures, concerts and exhibitions, while the recently restored mansion serves as a branch of the Glendale Public Library. The focus is art and music, with a circulating collection of framed prints. In the hills behind the house is a private cemetery where Mr. Brand is spending eternity in a pyramid.

....

1601 W Mountain St., Glendale, 91201
Tel: 818 548 2051
Tue: 12noon-8pm; Wed: 12noon-6pm;
Thu: 12noon-8pm; Fri-Sat: 10am-5pm

CASA BIANCA

Making the city's finest pizza since the 1950s, this place still draws a crowd. If the cramped inside waiting area is full, chairs are provided outside, and if that's too much to bear, you can call ahead and put your name on the list for a table. Appetisers include salads, fried mozzarella with tomato sauce, and fried zucchini spears with dipping sauce. The recommended rich pesto pizza takes an additional 20 minutes and there's molto fennel in that homemade sausage. Take note, it closes for a month or so in summer.

....

1650 Colorado Boulevard, 90041
Tel: 323 256 9617
Tue-Thu: 4pm-12midnight; Fri-Sat: 4pm-1am

FAIR OAKS PHARMACY AND SODA FOUNTAIN

There's been a drugstore at the corner of Mission and Fair Oaks since 1915; the soda fountain went in sometime in the 1930s and became a popular pit stop for folks arriving in Los Angeles on old Route 66. But over time, retail updates buried the vintage look. In the 1990s, then-owners Michael and Meredith Miller stripped the space back to the bones for a loving restoration, sourcing decorative elements from as far as Missouri. Today you can enjoy a phosphate, malt, root beer float, Thrifty brand ice cream sundae or lunch atop a tall stool. Plus retro candy and souvenirs, and yes, you can fill a prescription here.

....

1526 Mission St., South Pasadena, 91030
Tel: 626 799 1414
Mon-Sat: 9am-9pm; Sun: 10am-7pm

Fair Oaks Pharmacy And Soda Fountain

GLENDALE / EAGLE ROCK / PASADENA / SOUTH PASADENA

FOREST LAWN CEMETERY

The original cemetery as tourist attraction (1906) sprung fully formed from the mind of Dr. Hubert Eaton, the visionary early director. Eaton consolidated mortuary services with grave sales and eliminated the depressing stone gardens of upright monuments, but his real interest lay in turning the cemetery into a zone of culture and beauty, filled with original and replica artworks that he obtained from world's fairs and impoverished European collectors. Here you can stroll among stained glass windows depicting the founding of America, marry in a wee church copied stone by stone from the old world original, marvel at a 195-foot-long painting of the Crucifixion housed in a custom showroom and pay your respects to innumerable celebrated Angelenos who are spending eternity in these sweeping lawns.

1712 S GLENDALE AVE., GLENDALE, 91205
TEL: 323 254 3131
DAILY: 8AM-5PM

GUS'S BARBECUE

Just across from the 1925 Rialto Theatre — a picturesque, though shuttered, landmark — is a beloved bit of old South Pasadena that's kept up with the times. The original Gus's (opened 1946) was a dive bar and diner, formerly known as Hamburger Mac's. Brothers Chris and John Bicos bought the business in 2007 and gussied up the interior with a modern blues shack / sports bar vibe. More significantly, inspired by the barnyard creatures on the vintage neon sign, they laid in a smoker and crafted a menu that reads like a meat lover's road trip: Memphis, Texas, Saint Louis and South Carolina style BBQ are all represented.

808 FAIR OAKS AVE., SOUTH PASADENA, 91030
TEL: 626 799 3251
MON-THU: 11AM-10PM; FRI: 11AM-11PM;
SAT: 8.30AM-11PM; SUN: 8.30AM-10PM

HUNTINGTON DESERT GARDEN

It's an easy slur to suggest that Los Angeles is an improbable place for a great city, a desert plumped up with water stolen from Owens Valley farmers. In truth, our climate is the moister Mediterranean. Need proof? Head to the eastern end of this grand estate, where Henry E. Huntington's garden curator William Hertrich placed specimens of cactus, succulents, yuccas, agaves and bromeliads collected from all the world's arid places. Add more than a century of coddling and husbandry, and the result is an otherworldly forest of gigantic spiky wonders, far larger than they could grow in their challenging natural habitats. The Huntington also has great books and paintings, and a magnificent set of faux wood arbors, but if your time is short, consider the cactus.

1151 OXFORD ROAD, SAN MARINO, 91108
TEL: 626 405 2125
SAT: 10.30AM-4.30PM

Macy's (formerly Bullock's)

GLENDALE / EAGLE ROCK / PASADENA / SOUTH PASADENA

MACY'S (FORMERLY BULLOCK'S)

Although the upscale Bullock's chain is no more, its grandest post-war department store (1947) survives in fine fettle as a Macy's in the heart of Pasadena's South Lake Street shopping corridor. Architects Wurdeman and Becket were given complete control of the project to craft a machine age "store of tomorrow," with retail departments flowing together seamlessly. While the best preserved sections of the original store are the charming baby barber shop and the Children's Department kitted out like a vintage cruise ship with art deco ceiling murals and curved walls, there are original murals and display cases throughout the store. We know of no prettier place to buy a pair of socks.

.....

401 South Lake Ave., Pasadena, 91101
Tel: 626 792 0211
Mon-Fri: 10am-9pm; Sat: 10am-8pm; 11am-7pm

PASADENA US POST OFFICE

If you have to stand in line to mail a package, you may as well do it inside the most beautiful vintage post office in greater Los Angeles. Although this section of Pasadena's Colorado Boulevard suffered the ravages of 1970s redevelopment, the Beaux Arts post office (by Oscar Wenderoth, 1913) escaped unscathed. Notable features include fluted columns supporting a stained glass ceiling in delicate greens and yellows, elegant sorting tables, vintage metal clerk cages and post boxes. Unfortunately, the most beautiful post office is also among the most understaffed. But there's plenty of beauty to take in while you wait, and wait.

.....

281 E Colorado Boulevard, Pasadena, 91101
Tel: 626 744 0212
Mon-Fri: 9am-5pm; Sat: 9am-2pm

PIE 'N BURGER

Beloved by Caltech students and the wider community of serious hamburger fans, Pie 'n Burger has delivered its minimalist namesake menu, and a few sandwiches, protein salads and breakfast items, since 1963. Most patrons head straight for the counter, where the waitresses don't stare as thick rivulets of house made 1000 Island dressing drip from the quarter pound burgers, which are pricey but, some say, the best in town. The pies are also terrific, with about a dozen rotating flavours available daily, including year-round holiday pumpkin. Save room for a malt, blended while you watch on a vintage Hamilton Beach machine. Cash only. Pro tip: if the flag is flying outside, the wine shop in back is open.

.....

913 E California Boulevard, Pasadena, 91106
Tel: 626 795 1123
Mon-Fri: 6am-10pm; Sat: 7am-10pm;
Sun: 7am-9pm

Hollywood

101 COFFEE SHOP

From the late 1930s, the Hollywood Franklin Hotel operated a luncheonette/pharmacy/liquor store on the ground floor. Today the hotel is a Best Western and its retro-remodelled coffee shop with Flintstone walls and cosy booths, continues to attract a young bohemian Hollywood clientele, as it has done since the late 1940s. A film spools in the lobby exhaustively detailing both the hotel and luncheonette's history and famous patrons, and to underline the star connection, the walls are covered with framed autographed head shots. Menu standouts include the smoked chicken salad and French dip and grilled tandoori salmon sandwiches, plus the black eye milk shake with its shot of espresso.

6145 Franklin Ave., 90028 / Tel: 323 467 1175
Daily: 7am-3am

BOARDNER'S BAR

A quintessential dimly-lit, down-and-dirty serious drinking joint. After many other names and owners, Steve Boardner opened up in 1944 and the place has remained largely unchanged ever since. Besides being a favourite of working-class stiffs, its list of celebrity tipplers is long and varied, and includes Charles Bukowski, Errol Flynn, Lawrence Tierney, Ed Wood, Mickey Cohen and, accirding to in-house legend, even Elizabeth Short, the Black Dahlia herself. The bar's even done a bit of acting itself, notably in L.A. Confidential. Through the decades surrounding businesses have risen and fallen, but Boardner's remains with us.

1652 North Cherokee Ave., 90028
Tel: 323 462 9621
Daily: 5pm-2am

CANTER'S DELI

L.A.'s most famous deli serves up all the classics. Beginning in Boyle Heights, Canter's moved to North Fairfax in the late 1940s and was soon patronised by preening movie stars and spritzing comics. In 1953 it moved up the street and took over the old Esquire Theater, where it stands today. It has its own bakery and a full bar and lounge — The Kibitz Room, added in 1961. A big-time hang in the swingin' 1960s, when you might have caught Phil Spector ordering Lenny Bruce a Buck Benny hot dog. Eppis essen!

419 North Fairfax Ave., 90036
Tel: 323 651 2030
Daily: 24 hours (except Rosh Hashanah and Yom Kippur)

EL COYOTE CAFÉ

Here's a bit of old LA. trivia: the word "café" in an establishment's name means you can get a drink there — and El Coyote's margaritas are a big draw. Blanche and George March opened their original El Coyote in 1931; this branch and its neon dates to 1951. The multi-room complex is always busy, especially at Happy Hour, as waitresses in gaudy traditional costumes serve huge platters of Americanised Mexican food. True crime buffs revel in the fact that Sharon Tate and her houseguests ate their last meal here before encountering the Manson Family.

7312 Beverly Boulevard, 90036
Tel: 323 939 2255
Sun-Thu: 11.30am-10pm; Fri-Sat: 11.30am-11pm

THE ORIGINAL FARMER'S MARKET

Hold tight for a capsule history of Los Angeles development. When the Gilmore family settled this land in the 1870s, it was to raise dairy cattle. Later, they'd strike oil, build a speedway for midget motor races, host football and baseball games and sell chunks of the property to CBS Television and mall developer Rick Caruso. And in 1934, they welcomed farmers selling their wares from trucks in a fresh retail scheme conceived by Fred Beck and Roger Dahlhjelm. It was a smash, and within months permanent stalls were constructed for produce vendors, bakeries and butchers. Today it's a great place to grab a meal and watch the world go by. Vintage merchants include Du-Par's Restaurant, Bob's Donuts, Magee's Kitchen — the original market restaurant — and Patsy's Pizza, at the market since 1949, and supposedly L.A.'s first pizza (some contend it's still the best). Don't miss: the wee Gilmore Adobe (1828) in the centre of the property, best viewed from atop the parking structure.

6333 W 3rd St., 90036 / Tel: 323 933 9211
Mon-Fri: 9am-9pm; Sat: 9am-8pm; Sun: 10am-7pm

FORMOSA CAFÉ

This eatery was opened in the mid-1920s by a prize-fighter, inside an old red trolley car that remains part of the structure. The Chinese-style red and black interior is quite dark, its walls covered by old movie-star photos, due to its proximity to the United Artists / Goldwyn lot; patrons have included Humphrey Bogart, Marilyn Monroe and gangster Bugsy Siegel. Threatened by demolition in the 1990s, it survives as an unofficial landmark, suffering some recent, regrettable, alterations. Chinese food is still served but the bar is the chief draw.

7156 Santa Monica Boulevard, 90046
Tel: 323 850 9050
Mon-Fri: 4pm-2am; Sat-Sun: 6pm-2am

GILMORE GAS (STARBUCKS COFFEE SHOP)

To find old L.A., one typically steers away from corporate venues. But since 2015, in the heart of Hollywood, Starbucks Coffee has occupied a very cool structure. The wee 1930s-era Art Deco Gilmore Gas Station was a movie star — look for it in 48 Hours and L.A. Story — and a city landmark. But it had been shuttered and allowed to fall into disrepair. Enter the Seattle chain, which went above and beyond to tastefully reinvent the station as the most beautiful drive-in and walk-up coffee stand around. In a neighbourhood where many fine buildings have been lost, it seems a little miraculous.

859 N Highland Ave., 90038
Tel: 323 493 1868
Sun-Thu: 5am-10pm; Fri-Sat: 5am-11pm

GRAUMAN'S CHINESE THEATRE

For decades, tourists have flocked to the red pagoda exterior and star-studded forecourt sporting some 200 footprints, handprints and autographs of generations of Hollywood royalty. The interior retains much of its original plush chinoiserie, with upgraded digital projection gear. Be sure to check out the ornate restrooms.

6925 Hollywood Boulevard, 90028
Tel: 323 465 4847 / 464 8111

GRAUMAN'S EGYPTIAN THEATRE

The broad courtyard entrance has been restored to the 1922 original, but the remodeled pocket lobby has little Egyptiana remaining. Keep moving: the theatre ceiling, a gilded scarab for the ages.

6712 Hollywood Boulevard, 90028
Tel: 323 461 2020

HOLLYWOOD FOREVER CEMETERY

Opened in 1899, this is the final resting place of a number of early Tinseltown luminaries. Valentino is in one mausoleum along with Peter Lorre and director John Huston. Instigated by film society Cinespia in 2002, summer weekly screenings of classic movies are shown against the outside wall of a tomb. Gates open at 7pm, allowing plenty of time for audiences to find a spot to spread out their blankets and picnic before the movie begins. For the historically minded, Karie Bible's daytime walking tours are highly recommended.

6000 Santa Monica Boulevard, 90038
Tel: 323 469 1181
Daily: 7am-6pm

LARRY EDMUNDS BOOKSHOP

Strange as it sounds Hollywood Boulevard, now a lurid tourist trap where costumed beggars brawl for sidewalk space, was once one of the world's great bookstore districts. Pickwick, Cherokee, Book City, Larson's, Stanley Rose. Great stores with passionate owners, eccentric staff, and loyal clientele including the legendary novelists who'd come out west to slum for big bucks at Paramount, Warner's and Fox. Today, only one of the original Hollywood bookstores survives, but it's a doozy: our first and best entertainment memorabilia store (since 1938, though it was a literary bookshop for the first couple of decades), offering

Hollywood Forever Cemetery

NORMS

entertainers' biographies, screenwriting guides, vintage posters and fan magazines, postcards, paper dolls, 8 x 10 glossies and a terrific programme of in-store lectures and book signings. Long live The Lare!

6644 HOLLYWOOD BOULEVARD, 90028
TEL: 323 463 3273
MON-FRI: 10AM-5.30PM; SAT: 10AM-6PM;
SUN: 12NOON-5.30PM

LASKY-DEMILLE BARN

Tucked into the back of a surface parking lot opposite the Hollywood Bowl is one of early cinema's most storied structures, the barn rented by pioneering director Cecil B. DeMille and producing partner Jesse Lasky during the 1913 production of The Squaw Man, the first Hollywood-made feature. Originally situated at Selma and Vine, the old barn had been moved several times when it was acquired by the Hollywood Heritage preservation group, who turned it into a museum of early motion pictures, with a small bookshop and lecture hall. Its odd location is due to a legal case brought by Steve Anthony, whose nearby home was seized and demolished to build a larger cinema museum that never got off the ground.

2100 HIGHLAND AVE., HOLLYWOOD, 90068
TEL: 323 874 2276
WED-SUN: 12NOON-4PM

THE MAGIC CASTLE

One of the world's great private clubs, Hollywood's Magic Castle was founded in 1963 by brothers Milt and Bill Larsen as a place for their magician friends to congregate. It is still family run. The main structure was the Rollin B. Lane mansion (1909), but the club has expanded to encompass numerous performance spaces, dining rooms and bars, such fabulous bars. Much of the interior decoration was salvaged by Milt from 19th century buildings facing the wrecking ball; the gift shop carries a book documenting his finds. Guests can enjoy some of the world's top illusionists in shows small and grand and running all night. Off the restaurant-level bar, a ghostly pianist named Irma plays requests for tips. Not a member? Book a night next door at the Magic Hotel, or request a pass from a magician on the Castle's website calendar whose show you'd like to catch.

7001 FRANKLIN AVE., 90028 / TEL: 323 851 3313
MON-WED: 5PM-2AM; THU-FRI: 4.45PM-2AM;
SAT-SUN: 10AM-3PM & 4.45PM-2AM

MICELI'S

Beginning life as Miceli's Pizzaria (sic) in 1949 with recipes from Sicily by way of Chicago, this Hollywood mainstay is still owned by the same family. Legend has it that Steve Boardner of Boardner's Bar (see page 38) gave Carmen Miceli $400 to buy the place. Some of the furnishings come

HOLLYWOOD

from another old Hollywood eatery, the Pig 'n' Whistle (recently reopened in its original location next to the old Egyptian Theatre, see page 36). Miceli's serves solid traditional food from The Boot, with live music most nights; the great jazz trumpeter and vocalist Jack Sheldon recently held down a regular gig here.

1646 North Las Palmas Ave., 90028
Tel: 323 466 3438
Sun-Thu: 11.30am-11pm;
Fri-Sat: 11.30am-12midnight

MOUN OF TUNIS

L.A.'s original Tunisian restaurant since 1977, Moun (pronounced "moon") of Tunis is, quite simply, a trip. Guests pass through keyhole doorways to sit cross-legged on Persian carpets in rooms draped with colourful fabrics and illuminated by hanging lamps. Hands are cleansed at the table by waiters bearing jugs of rose water. The richly spiced food is served family style on brass chargers. Periodically, limber belly dancers appear and do extraordinary things with their bejeweled anatomies. Meals conclude with mint tea and the ritual lounging back on pillows and opening up of top trouser buttons. Fun fact: the door is in the back of the building, on a diagonal alley that was originally a right of way for L.A.'s lost streetcars.

7445½ Sunset Boulevard, 90046
Tel: 323 874 3333
Daily: 5pm-11pm

MUSSO & FRANK GRILL

Flannel cakes, welsh rarebit, crab louie salad and sauerbraten on Wednesdays are but some of the perennial favourites at this most hallowed, never remodelled, watering hole. The dimly lit "old room" to the west dates from 1934. The new room, from 1954, has the former (now closed) back-room bar where many a Tinseltown scribe — Chandler, Faulkner, Fitzgerald et al — did irreparable damage to their livers with icy martinis and other potent potables. The menu's offerings, if not its prices, remain largely unchanged from its 1919 inception.

6667 Hollywood Boulevard, 90028
Tel: 323 467 7788
Tue-Sat: 11am-11pm

NORMS LA CIENEGA

Starting in 1949, Norm Roybark launched a chain of Southern California casual dining restaurants distinguished by their high modern architecture and devotion to quality ingredients and friendly service, 24 hours a day, seven days a week. The oldest surviving Norms is this 1957 beauty with its saw-toothed pennant blade sign, designed by Googie giants Louis Armet and Eldon Davis and winner of the National Restaurant Association's design award. Named a city landmark in 2015 after new landlords threatened to turn it into a retail boutique, this busy Norms remains an anchor of the Hollywood

Vedanta Society of Southern California

community. Stop in for an only-in-L.A. aesthetic and culinary experience while you still can.

470 La Cienega Boulevard, 90048
Tel: 310 657 8333
Daily: 24 hours

VEDANTA SOCIETY OF SOUTHERN CALIFORNIA

The Ramakrishna Order monk and philosopher Swami Prabhavananda came to Los Angeles in 1929, establishing his monastery on a hill overlooking Hollywood. Here he found a community of Western thinkers hungry for Eastern enlightenment. Vedanta became a spiritual home for expatriate authors Christopher Isherwood, Aldous Huxley and Gerald Heard, who popularised Prabhavananda's ideas through their work. Prabhavananda died in 1976, but his Hollywood ashram lives on, with its beautiful white domed temple like a miniature Taj Mahal and fine spiritual bookshop housed in a Craftsman bungalow. Although the noisy Hollywood Freeway (1947) passes quite close to the property, Vedanta remains a peaceful space where spiritual seekers are always welcome for daily worship and meditation services, Sunday lectures or simply to enjoy the garden.

1946 Vedanta Place, Hollywood, 90068
Tel: 323 465 7114
Daily: 6.30am-7pm

WATTLES PARK

How about a Hollywood hills hike with a side of Old L.A.? Then skip crowded Runyon Canyon and take a walk on the Wattles side. On Curson Avenue just north of Hollywood Boulevard is "Jualita" (architects Myron Hunt and Elmer Grey), the Mission Revival mansion constructed as a winter home for Omaha banker Gurdon Wattles in 1907. The city-owned property, restored by Hollywood Heritage, is the last survivor of the original Hollywood estates, all long since subdivided for housing or commercial use. The mansion's lower orchards are now a community garden, and behind it is a steep grassy park that feeds into hiking trails above. The house is rarely open save as a wedding venue, but the exterior can be viewed from the park.

1850 N Curson Ave., 90046 / Tel: 323 666 5046
Daily: Dawn to dusk

Mid-city

MID-CITY

ALVARADO TERRACE

Ah, the Pico-Union district, rough and tumble and full of excitement, home to excellent hole-in-the-wall Salvadoran joints, a thriving sidewalk vending scene and some world-class fake IDs. And just around the corner from the Salvation Army thrift shop, a startling half-moon of six landmark mansions, developed between 1902-05. The houses are a miniature National Register Historic District and a lesson in how quickly high architectural fashion can shift: Craftsman-Tudor (Boyle-Barmore House) to Shingle Style (Cohn House) to Mission Revival (Powers House). The strip of grass in the centre of the street was originally a park, with on-site gardener and koi pond. And that tiny section of bricked roadway is L.A.'s shortest street, just 15 feet long. Squint just right, and it's like the 20th century never happened.

Corner of Pico Boulevard and Alvarado Street

BOB BAKER MARIONETTE THEATER

Just west of Downtown, tucked under a bridge and atop the celebrated Edward Doheny oil strike, the city's longest continuously operating children's theatre continues to delight with matinee performances of the sly, silly and sometimes sexy musical productions that founder Baker (1924-2014) created in the 1960s. Kids big and small sprawl on the red carpet to get an up close experience

La Brea Tar Pits

HOW TO FIND OLD LOS ANGELES

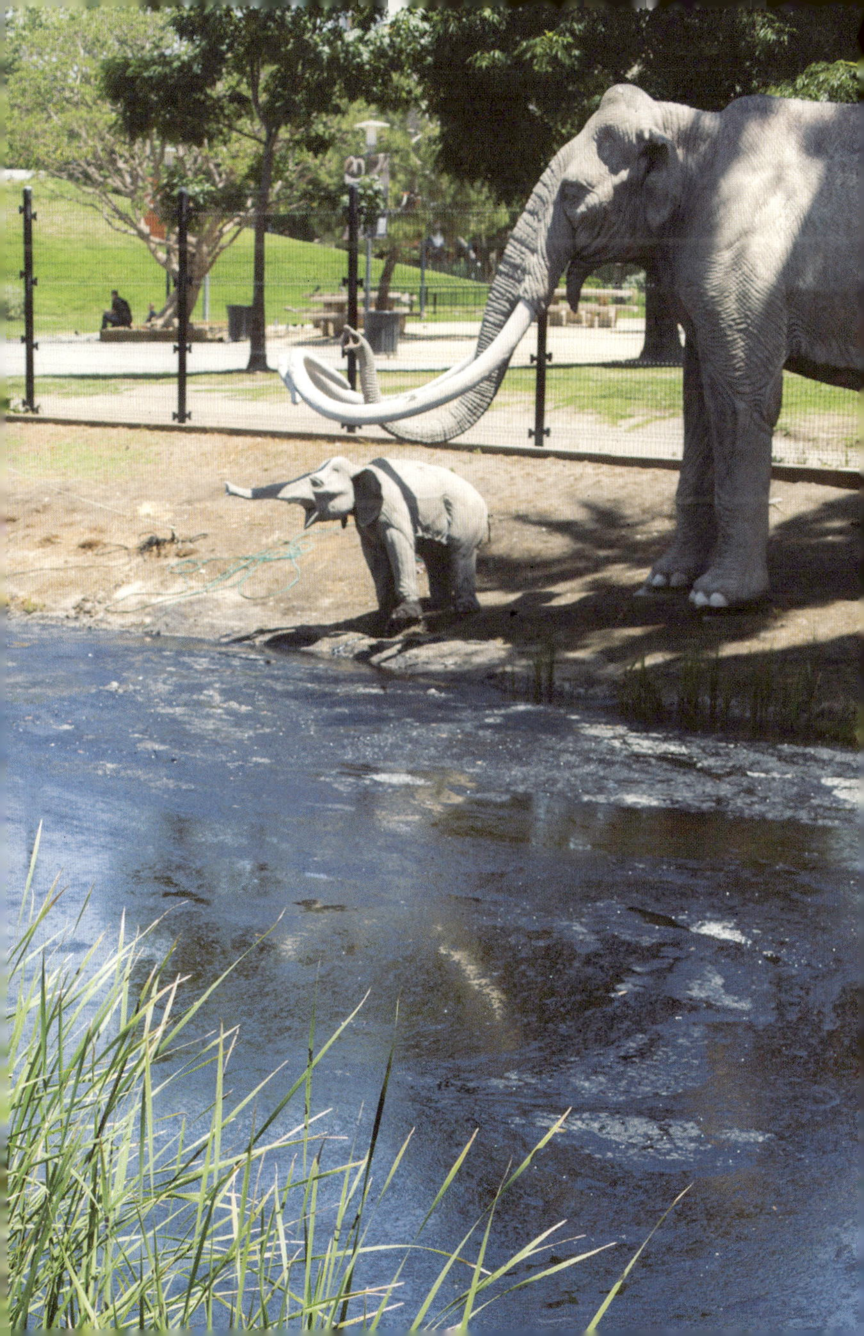

Pacific Dining Car

with giant stringed creatures that just might sit on your lap, if you're good. After the show, guests enjoy complementary ice cream in the candy-coloured party room. Although a city landmark, this beloved time capsule is in a developer's crosshairs. Experience it while you can.

1345 W 1st St., 90026 / Tel: 213 250 9995

EL CHOLO

Starting life as the Sonora Café in 1923, this large and most renowned of L.A.'s traditional Mexican restaurants got a name change a few years later, moved a few years after that, before finally settling across Western Avenue in 1931. It continued to expand until the 1970s and today there are several colourfully decorated dining rooms — the older, smaller ones with high-backed wood booths are recommended. The famous green corn tamales are served from May to October, but the strong Margaritas, and muy sabroso chimichangas, are always available.

1121 South Western Ave., 90006
Tel: 323 734 2773
Mon-Thu: 11am-10pm; Fri-Sat: 11am-11pm;
Sun: 11am-9pm

H.M.S. BOUNTY

Located across the street from the site of the now-demolished Ambassador Hotel, this was the spot where all the journalists hung out in the aftermath of Bobby Kennedy's assassination in June 1968. Opened six years earlier, each booth in the bar room has a brass plaque identifying it as the favourite of a past patron. Choose from Walter Winchell, Jack Webb or Winston Churchill (among others) before ordering one of their tasty grilled pepper jack cheese sandwiches and a glass of beer. Full-course dinners are served in the adjoining restaurant.

3357 Wilshire Boulevard, 90010
Tel: 213 385 7275
Sun-Thu: 11pm-1am; Fri-Sat: 11pm-2am

LA BREA TAR PITS

It doesn't get much more Old L.A. than the last ice age, when extinct megafauna with jazzy names like dire wolf, saber-toothed cat and mastodon ambled along the dirt trail that we know today as Wilshire Boulevard. Sometimes they'd stop to drink at cool reflecting pools, unaware that beneath the sheen of rainwater lurked pits of deadly, semi-liquid oil. Thousands of animals were trapped and sank beneath the surface, where their bones turned to stone. Today, you can peep into the working excavation pits where paleontologists painstakingly extract interesting bits from the tar matrix, or tour the 1960s-era Page Museum with its world class fossil collection. But be alert while roaming the park grounds: tar continues to bubble up through the earth, and while you're unlikely to be trapped, you might just wreck your sneakers.

5801 Wilshire Boulevard, 90036
Tel: 213 763 3499
Daily: 9.30am-5pm

LANGER'S DELI

With the possible exception of Schwartz's in Montreal, this beloved 1940s noshery serves the best pastrami on rye in North America. A statement to which, with the demise of several lamented New York City meccas, even an east-coaster like the late Nora Ephron concurred. Given its historic-but-grubby MacArthur Park neighbourhood, this bastion of Jewish bar-b-q got a fresh lease of life because the subway now stops just a block away. Decor is deli basic with booths. Go for the pastrami-and-corned-beef combo, tell 'em to make it all pastrami and share with a friend. Free refills on the great-tasting homemade cream soda, plus free parking on the next block.

704 South Alvarado St., 90057
Tel: 213 483 8050
Mon-Sat: 8am-4pm

NATURAL HISTORY MUSEUM & EXPOSITION PARK ROSE GARDEN

Early Angelenos flocked down Grasshopper Street (now Figueroa) to visit Agricultural Park (1871-1911), anything goes zone of sport and pleasure. The seven-acre sunken rose gardens were planted in 1927, and are on the National Register. Inhale the heady perfume and imagine what sins this site has seen. At the west end of the garden is the County's original 1913 museum building (originally dedicated to art and history, too), with its exquisite Judson glass domed rotunda, home to Julia Bracken Wendt's "Three Muses" sculpture. The museum also contains vintage large mammal taxidermy halls (1920s) and an important collection of local history artifacts.

900 Exposition Boulevard, 90007
Tel: 213 763 3466
Daily: 9.30am-5pm

NICK'S COFFEE SHOP

What a local eatery should be: family owned, friendly to all, mid-20th century designed, quick service at booth or counter, with consistently tasty and generous portions of calorific comfort food on offer. Signed head shots of assorted smiling mummers share wall space with quirky family mementos in this diner with salt, pepper and Lawry's Seasoned Salt shakers on every table. Outside dining in warm weather. They do a fine patty melt and the extensive menu has a plethora of choices — all good. It can get crowded at peak hours.

8536 West Pico Boulevard, 90035
Tel: 310 652 3567
Daily: 7.30am-3pm

ORIGINAL TOMMY'S HAMBURGERS

Longtime Angelenos know, if they're feeling lonesome at 3 in the morning, they can go to the corner of Beverly and Rampart and find a crowd. There's always a quick-moving line at Tom Koulax's original burger shack outpost, which has pumped out uncountable chili dogs and chili burgers since 1946. Tommy's got so popular in the 1960s that Koulax expanded, putting in a larger L-shaped restaurant and some parking, and in recent years branches have opened across California and into Nevada. But for the vintage experience, place your order at the wee shack at the corner of Beverly and Rampart, pocket some paper napkins and eat right there on the sidewalk.

2575 W Beverly Boulevard, 90057
Tel: 213 389 9060
Daily: 24 hours

PACIFIC DINING CAR

L.A.'s civic leaders and legal lights have been breaking bread at this fancy 24-hour citadel since 1921. It was redesigned in a comfortable mid-century style during 1960, with the original train car only part of the whole. Although not cheap, the service and food are consistently excellent whether you go for the famous breakfasts, late-night repasts or anything in between. Renowned as a great steakhouse, their corn-fed beef is aged on the premises and they make their own signature steak sauce. Extensive wine selection.

1310 West 6th St., 90017 / Tel: 213 483 6000
Daily: 24 hours

Tom Bergin's Public House

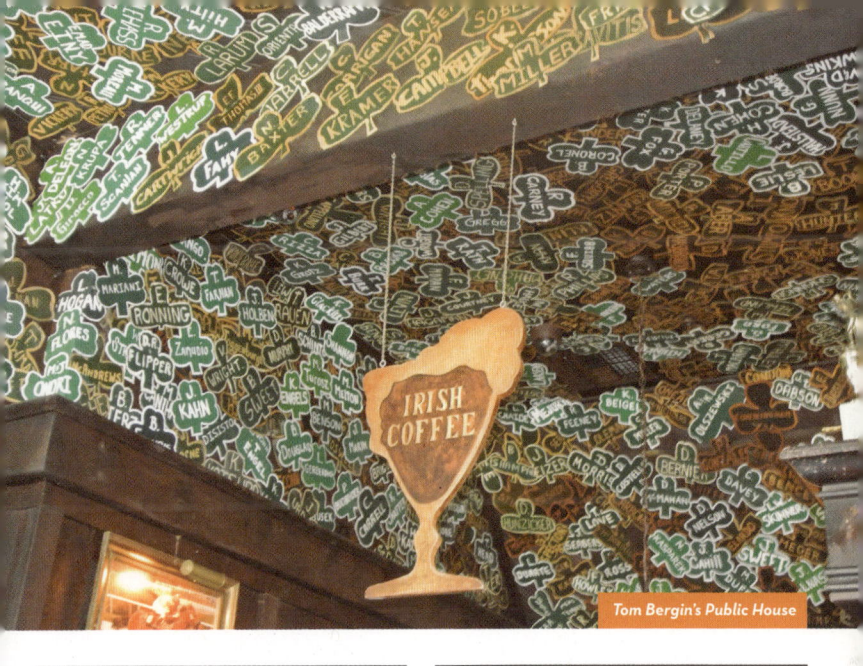

PAPA CRISTO'S

In 1948, Greek immigrant Sam Chrys founded C & K Importing to bring traditional foods and wine to the American market. Twenty years later, Sam's son Chrys expanded the thriving business to include a small restaurant, later an old world taverna with rows of communal tables. Sundays are especially busy, as many Greek Angelenos come back to the old neighbourhood to attend services at St. Sophia Cathedral and stock up on staples. The no-frills market section is still much as it was when Sam unpacked his first crate of feta.

2771 W Pico Boulevard, 90006
Tel: 323 737 2970
Tue: 9.30am-3pm; Wed-Sat: 9.30-8pm;
Sun: 9am-4pm

PINK'S HOT DOGS

L.A.'s most famous wiener stand, outlasting the now-defunct Tail-Of-The-Pup and The Dog House chain. There seems to have been a fast-moving line for chili dogs with mustard and onions since 1939. Once a favourite of the gaggle of studio musicians known as the Wrecking Crew, who would refuel here after a long gruelling session at Gold Star Studios. On drummer Hal Blaine's 1966 instrumental Midnight At Pink's someone in the background, after one dog too many, can be heard asking for bicarbonate of soda.

709 North La Brea Ave., 90038
Tel: 323 931 4223
Sun-Thu: 9.30am-2am; Fri-Sat: 9.30am-3am

HOW TO FIND OLD LOS ANGELES

MID-CITY

THE PRINCE

Formerly The Windsor, where white-gloved waiters served veal Oscar and other mid-century delights, it once shared the L.A. culinary firmament with Perrino's and Romanoff's. Housed in a corner of the 1927 Windsor apartment complex, the restaurant's original 1949 decor of murky oil paintings above mismatched brass plaques, semi-circular wall booths with buzzers to bring the wait staff, inset next to kitschy figure lamps of lords and tipplers remains untouched. There's also a heraldic room and bar in the back for private parties. After closing in 1991 it reopened as a Korean restaurant specialising in fried chicken and it's a real kick to sit among the Hollywood ghosts, dipping crispy pieces of bird in rice wraps into hot sauce while listening to the Beach Boys mellow out over the radio on Good Vibrations.

3198 1/2 WEST 7TH ST., 90005
TEL: 213 389 1586 / 2007
DAILY: 4PM-2AM

TAYLOR'S STEAKHOUSE

Originally known as Taylor's Tavern when it opened in 1953, it eventually became a full-on surf 'n' turf destination before moving to its present location in 1970. One large dining room on the second floor, and a slightly smaller one with a single long table off the downstairs main room make it a favourite for hosting private parties. The various cuts of meat are priced reasonably, while their signature Molly salad of blue cheese, beefsteak tomato and iceberg lettuce is a popular starter.

3361 WEST 8TH ST., 90005
TEL: 213 382 8449
MON-THU: 11.30AM-9.30PM; FRI: 11.30AM-10.30PM;
SAT: 4PM-10.30PM; SUN: 4PM-9.30PM

TOM BERGIN'S PUBLIC HOUSE

A few years ago, fans feared the number was up for the venerable "House of Irish Coffee" (established 1936, at this location since 1949). A new owner came in with plans to upgrade, overextended himself, then shuttered the bar in a huff. The fretful didn't reckon on how much the mid-Wilshire community loves their local. Neighbour Derek Schreck purchased the bar and undid the unwelcome, and happily superficial, changes. The ceiling above the famous Horseshoe Bar is still coated with paper shamrocks inscribed with patrons' names, including some familiar from the entertainment world. The regulars still hold up the bar. And it's still the place to be on Saint Patrick's Day, or any time you crave a shot of Jameson's in your java.

840 S. FAIRFAX AVE., 90036 / TEL: 323 936 7151
MON-THU: 5PM-2AM; FRI-SAT: 11AM-2AM;
SUN: 11AM-11PM

San Fernando Valley

SAN FERNANDO VALLEY

THE BEAR PIT BAR-B-Q

In the late 1940s, Ben Baier brought his native Missouri-style barbeque to the wilds of Newhall, moving to this site several years later. Through several owners, the Pit's gustatory charms have remained constant: giant slabs of oven-smoked meat drenched in sweet sauce offset by the vinegary tang of the coleslaw, roomy tables for family style feasting and sawdust on the floor so nobody feels bad for dripping. With the vintage neon sign buzzing above the cute country cabin packed with happy diners, this San Fernando Valley landmark is worth the detour. Bottled sauce is available for purchase.

10825 Sepulveda Boulevard, Mission Hills, 91345 / Tel: 818 365 2500
Sun-Thu: 11.30am-9pm; Fri-Sat: 11.30am-10pm

GRANDMA PRISBREY'S BOTTLE VILLAGE

Soon after Tressa Prisbrey settled in remote Simi Valley in 1946, she began bringing useful things home from the dump. First glass bottles, which she mortared together into a neat little house to hold her vast pencil collection. Then discarded baby dolls, staked upright like flowers in a garden. Into the early 1980s and her old age, Tressa crafted mosaic floors and walls packed with personal symbolism and jewel-like bottle houses to hold her treasures. When she deeded the site to preservationists, it was recognised as one of America's great folk art environments. The unreinforced buildings fared poorly in the Northridge earthquake, and the landmark is only occasionally opened for tours, but you can see a lot of beauty from the property line.

4595 Cochran St., Simi Valley, 93062
Tel: 805 231 2497
Tours available

THE IDLE HOUR

The Idle Hour Café opened in 1941, its unique architecture — a giant beer barrel flanked by vats — announcing it to all who passed as a fine place to get a drink. From 1972-83 it was Dolores Fernandez' flamenco bar, La Caña. Miss Fernandez closed the business and lived out her days in the barrel, which became pretty dilapidated. After her death, bar developers 1933 Group swept in to restore the Idle Hour to its original splendor, and then some. Out back, you can sit in a wee replica of another famous programmatic structure, a café shaped like a bulldog, while nibbling house smoked brisket and enjoying an adult beverage.

4824 Vineland Ave., North Hollywood, 91601
Tel: 818 980 5604
Mon: 5pm-2am; Tue-Sun: 11am-2am

IDLE HOUR

Tally Rand

THE SMOKE HOUSE RESTAURANT

You've got to cross over the Hollywood Hills into Burbank to find one of the motion picture industry's greatest culinary time capsules. An easy amble from Warner Brothers Studios and always popular with movie folks, the Smoke House was founded in 1946. In 1948, it moved into down the street to its present location, a rambling half-timbered, faux country inn built by comic Danny Kaye. Sink into one of the deep, red pleated booths among the dark wood paneling and soak up the unchanged mid-century atmosphere with a side of the famous garlic toast. Popular times to visit: weekday afternoon happy hours and Sunday's seafood-heavy buffet brunch.

4420 Lakeside Drive, Burbank, 91505
Tel: 818 845 3731
Mon-Thu: 11.30am-10pm; Fri-Sat: 11.30am-11pm;
Sun: 10am-9pm

TALLY RAND

The menu says Tallyrand, but the gleaming backlit plastic sign on the mod, mansard roof begs to differ (Tally Rand). To further the nomenclature uncertainty, Al and Delores Thomas titled their 1959 coffee shop after a soup honoring French statesman Charles Maurice de Talleyrand. Well, you say tomato, I say tomahto. What matters is that Burbankites of a certain age love the rich comfort food, big booths for lounging, counter service for solo diners and the cocktail lounge. Shortly before his death, California chronicler Huell Howser filmed an episode of his popular TV show here, making the signature hot turkey sandwich forever after Huell's Special. Other specialties: pancakes, cinnamon French toast, oven-roasted turkey dinners.

1700 W Olive Ave., Burbank, 91506
Tel: 818 846 9904
Sun-Mon: 6am-9pm; Tue-Sat: 6am-10pm

San Gabriel Valley

SAN GABRIEL VALLEY

BROGUIERE'S FARM FRESH DAIRY

What's more old school American cool than creamy milk served from an icy glass bottle, the kind that was once delivered by the milkman in his natty white work gear? Home delivery is a thing of the distant past, but you can still patronise Southern California's last surviving family-run drive-in dairy store (since 1920), where locals stock up on low-priced eggs, breakfast cereal and big bottles of the good stuff. Look for the giant black and white cow next to the retro roof sign and the vintage delivery truck parked on the lawn, and be sure to try the eggnog around the holidays. Their slogan: "Milk so Fresh, the Cow Doesn't Know it's Missing."

505 S Maple Ave., Montebello, 90640
Tel: 323 726 0524
Mon-Fri: 7am-7pm; Sat: 7am-6pm; Sun: 8am-2pm

BUN 'N BURGER

The city of Alhambra has been experiencing a glut of redevelopment and doesn't landmark historic buildings, which makes the survival of this perfect sea-foam green 1941 diner with its exuberant running chef neon sign all the more remarkable. But Bun 'N Burger isn't going anywhere, if its many regulars have anything to say about it. Every spare inch of wall space is decorated with nostalgic items, many brought in by customers: vintage Coca-Cola signs, license plates, old newspapers and movie posters. Take a seat at the counter and enjoy generous servings of Mexican and American comfort food at a very nice price.

1000 E Main St., Alhambra, 91801
Tel: 626 281 6777
Mon-Tue: 6.30am-5.30pm; Wed: 6.30am-7pm; Thu: 6.30am-5.30pm; Fri-Sat: 6.30am-7pm; Sun: 7am-5pm

CLEARMAN'S STEAK 'N STEIN

John Foley Clearman was a Yale-trained thespian whose chosen form of theater was the whimsical, thematic steakhouse. Today you can still visit a Clearman's Northwoods Inn, with their fake snow on the roof and cosy hunting lodge decor, in the cities and San Gabriel, Covina or La Mirada. But there's only one Steak 'n Stein, the maestro's original establishment (1946). The style here is vintage East Coast roadhouse, with sandblasted brick and neon swinging in a wooden frame. Relax around the circular fire pit in the rustic lounge while perusing the mid-century menu. Meaty entrées come with potato, onion rings and cheese bread for the complete pre-Lipitor experience.

9545 E Whittier Boulevard, Pico Rivera, 90660
Tel: 562 699 8823
Mon-Thu: 11.30am-9pm; Fri-Sat: 11.30am-10pm; Sun: 10am-9pm

BUN N BURGER

SAN GABRIEL VALLEY

THE DAL RAE

The last branch standing in a wee 1950s Southland steakhouse chain, Dal Rae takes it name from founders Ed Dalton and Rae Harris, who soon sold to Ben and Bill Smith; the restaurant remains in the Smith family. Although purists lament the recent replacement of the vintage neon sign with a backlit plastic replica, Dal Rae remains a retro dining (and boozing) destination, with plush banquettes, wood paneling, white tablecloths and theatrical tableside preparation of generously proportioned classics like Steak Diane, Caesar Salad and Bananas Foster. The scallion-bacon-pepper-topped Pepper Steak is the specialty of the house.

9023 E. WASHINGTON BOULEVARD, PICO RIVERA, 90660 / TEL: 562 949 2444
MON-FRI: 11AM-4PM & 5PM-10PM;
SAT-SUN: 5PM-10PM

THE DERBY RESTAURANT

Should things go your way at Santa Anita racetrack, do as generations of winners have done and treat yourself to a fancy steak dinner at one of the region's oldest white linen restaurants. Originally known as Proctor's Tavern (1922), it moved to its present location in 1931. From 1938 until his fatal 1946 Santa Anita race, a co-owner was champion jockey George Woolf; legend holds he haunts the restaurant. It was under Woolf's ownership that the name was changed to honour the Kentucky Derby and the fabulous derby hat neon sign was installed. The homey space with its multiple dining rooms still displays some of Woolf's personal racing memorabilia. Solid Continental-American fare, heavy on the meat and butter.

233 E HUNTINGTON DRIVE, ARCADIA, 91006
TEL: 626 447 2430
MON-THU: 11.30AM-10PM; FRI: 11.30AM-11PM;
SAT: 4PM-11PM; SUN: 4PM-9PM

DIVINE'S FURNITURE

Monterey Park is a small city in transition, one of the largest suburban "New Chinatowns" that grew after the 1965 Immigration Act allowing Chinese residents to bring their extended families to America. While best known today as a foodie hotspot, offering every variety of dumpling, noodle, steamed bun and whole braised creature with the head still on, Monterey Park also boasts an excellent antique furniture shop. Divine's is the city's oldest continuously operating family business (since 1932), housed in a massive open air warehouse originally built by Japanese farmers to sell their crops. Colourful third-generation owner Chris Horn is the go-to guy for old San Gabriel Valley families when it's time to liquidate an estate or outfit a young couple just starting out. Prices are reasonable for solid pieces that will last a lifetime and the stock changes often.

802 E GARVEY AVE., MONTEREY PARK, 91755
TEL: 626 280 8484 / 323 283 8000
MON-SAT: 8AM-5PM

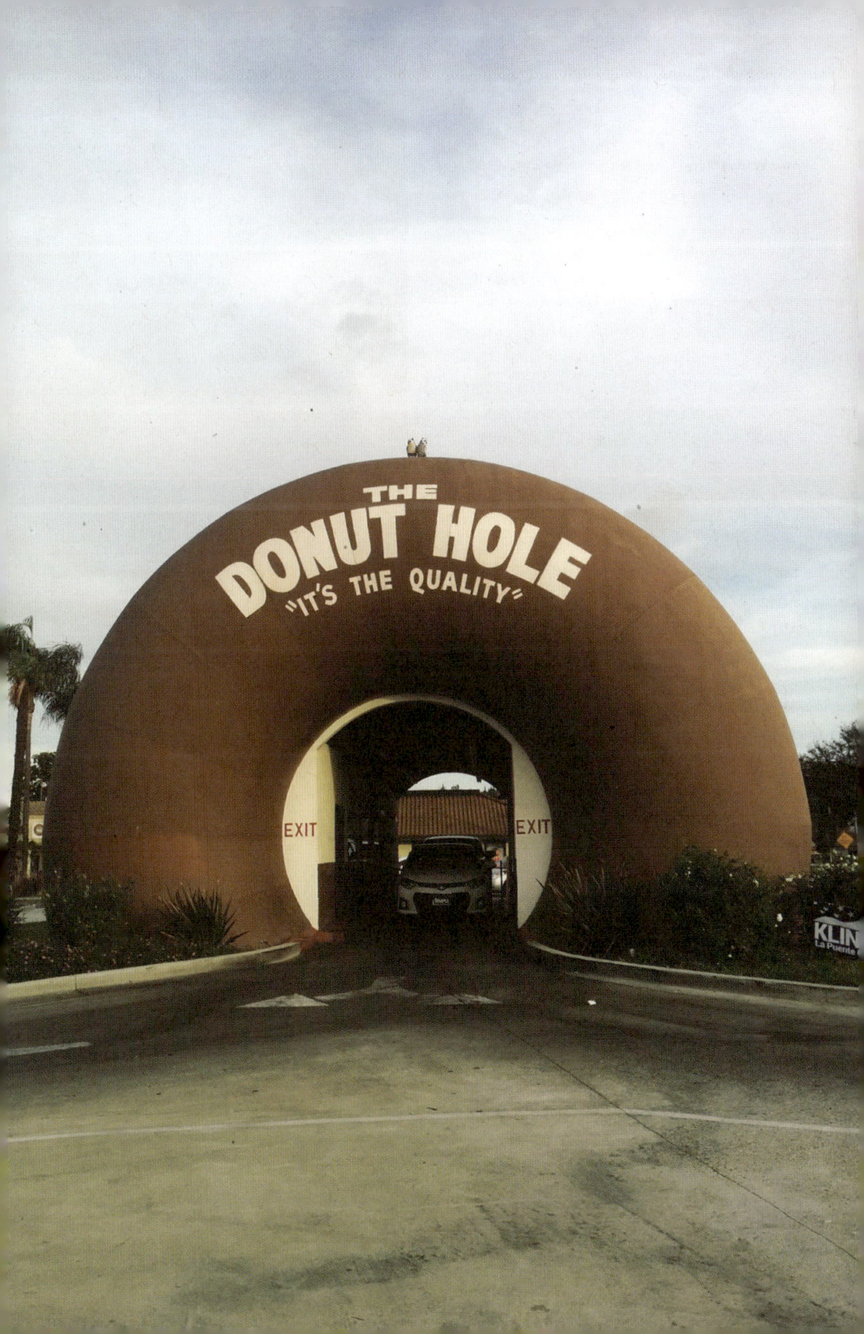
THE
DONUT HOLE
"IT'S THE QUALITY"
EXIT
EXIT

SAN GABRIEL VALLEY

THE DONUT HOLE

There are several giant donut establishments scattered around the southland, but only one that invites a patron to drive or walk right into the hole and out the other end. In the middle of the massive confection (a local landmark since 1968), just stop and tell the clerk what you're craving. In addition to traditional donut flavours, coffee, cocoa and juice, they offer trendy cronuts, red velvet, breakfast cereal- and bacon-topped donuts, plus a giant chocolate ring that mimics the design of the building. Be warned: every donut from the Donut Hole is a little bigger than an ordinary donut.

11332 Washington Boulevard, Whittier, 90606
Tel: 562 699 4138
Daily: 12noon-2am

THE EMBERS LOUNGE

A friendly, affordable Whittier dive bar that packs an art historical punch. The back of the bar is decorated with a jaw-dropping mural by Frank Howard Bowers (1905-1964) depicting busty lassies and libertines partying in fiery pits of Hades; similar works hang in frames around the room. Legend has it that the artist was a boozer who traded his art work for an open tab, but the gorgeous composition shows no sign of DTs or haste. Frank Bowers murals can still be found in several Southland taverns (the diviest being the Foc'scle longshoreman's joint in Wilmington), but for his last and most outrageous bar room composition, we're sending Old L.A. seekers straight to hell.

11332 Washington Boulevard, Whittier, 90606
Tel: 562 699 4138
Daily: 12noon-2am

FOSSELMAN'S

The Fosselman family makes simply great ice cream: dense, creamy, not too sweet. And in their picture perfect ice cream

Los Angeles County Arboretum and Botanic Garden

parlour and penny candy store at the end of Alhambra's main drag, they serve up all the classic concoctions like banana splits, root beer floats, malts and hot fudge sundaes to a steady stream of customers from morning to night. Peek through the front window to see the ice cream being churned on site. Along the walls, vintage photos and antique creamery tools celebrate the brand's deep San Gabriel Valley history (since 1919). But some new flavours with an Asian twist (taro, macapuno) show how the company is adapting to Alhambra's changing demographics. Why not mix it up with a scoop of lychee ice cream with butterscotch sauce?

1824 W Main St., Alhambra, 91801
Tel: 626 282 6533
Mon-Sat: 10am-10pm; Sun: 11.30am-10pm

THE HAT

Look for the neon chef's hat on a pole. In a retail zone that has otherwise become almost entirely Asian, an original bit of mid-century San Gabriel Valley fast food culture thrives. The Hat chain would ultimately number nine food stands, but this is the original (1951). The signature sandwich is the pastrami dip, a gooey mass of peppery thin-cut pink meat on a bun that will dissolve in your hands if you dilly-dally. Open until 1am seven nights a week, it's a great spot for a little something to tide you over till breakfast. Be warned: portions are huge, so note the half sandwich option.

1 W Valley Boulevard, Alhambra, 91801
Tel: 626 282 0140
Daily: 9am-1am

LOS ANGELES COUNTY ARBORETUM AND BOTANIC GARDEN

Elias Jackson "Lucky" Baldwin (1828-1909) was true to his nickname, a real estate speculator whose fortune ballooned though a series of improbable Gold Rush-era transactions. In 1875, bored with business and his first marriage, he picked up a modest spread in the San Gabriel Valley, the 13,000 acre Rancho Santa Anita. Baldwin transformed the old Spanish land grant into a Victorian paradise, its centrepiece a spring-fed artesian lake reflecting an exquisite Queen Anne mansion, which you might recognise from Fantasy Island. Nearby, perhaps the most luxurious horse barn and matching dog house ever constructed. Baldwin's real estate holdings were sold off and subdivided after his death, but 127 acres survive as this lovely public garden and concert venue, with its famous wandering peafowl, descendents of Baldwin's flock, and thousands of specimen plants and trees.

301 N Baldwin Ave., Arcadia, 91007
Tel: 626 821 3222
Daily: 9am-4.30pm

MARY'S MARKET & CANYON CAFÉ

In the winding hills above Sierra Madre, that perfect all-American town swarmed by pod people in Invasion of the Body Snatchers, you'll find a bustling diner inside an historic house. There's been a market here since 1922, catering to cabin residents along the Little Santa Anita Creek and folks bound for hiking excursions in the San Gabriels. The Sierra Madre hills have since become a neighbourhood with a Bohemian tinge. These days, the market is a home-style breakfast and lunch spot, offering egg dishes, hot and cold sandwiches, good coffee and occasional jam sessions by local players. Don't miss the photo wall.

561 Woodland Drive, Sierra Madre, 91024
Tel: 626 355 4534
Tue-Fri: 7.30am-7pm; Sat: 8am-6pm;
Sun: 8am-1.30pm

OCEANIC ARTS

The exotic Polynesian-inspired tiki scene flourished in the backyards and taverns of 1960s Los Angeles in no small part

Rod's Grill

due to the efforts of Oceanic Arts proprietors LeRoy Schmaltz (the artist) and Robert Van Oosting (the business guy). And you can still browse their 10,000 square foot workshop and warehouse today, picking out just the right tongue-lolling household god to make your very own tiki corner come alive. The stock includes luau accoutrements ranging from hanging glass fish net floats to rolls of woven matting, varnished puffer fish to flaming torches, floral lei necklaces to complete bamboo bar sets with matching stools. Large scale props, including man-sized tikis and acres of fishing nets, can be rented for special events.

12414 Whittier Boulevard, Whittier, 90602
Tel: 562 698 6960
Mon-Fri: 8am-4pm; Sat: 10am-1pm

ROD'S GRILL

Not far from historic Route 66 and Santa Anita racetrack is one of the Southland's most perfectly preserved Googie diners, cute enough to have played a Howard Johnson's on Mad Men. American and Mexican fare is cooked fresh to order, portions are generous and the price is nice. Rod's — a local chain operating since 1946, though this building is circa 1950s — is especially precious because it was nearly lost to eminent domain in 2006, when the Mercedes dealership next door tried to get the city to seize the land for a parking lot. Longtime waitress Julie organised a petition campaign that saved her job, and a beloved community gathering spot. Hop onto one of the teal stools at the counter and soak up the sweet smell of beating city hall.

41 W Huntington Drive, Arcadia, 91007
Tel: 626 447 7515
Daily: 6am-9pm

SANTA ANITA PARK

California's first (and L.A.'s last) thoroughbred racetrack opened in 1934 on land where millionaire sportsman "Lucky" Baldwin ran his ponies in the 'oughts. Architect Gordon Kaufmann was responsible for the eclectic Streamline Moderne / Colonial Revival design, which along with the San Gabriel Mountain views made a photo perfect backdrop for the Hollywood stars who frequented this pleasure palace in mid-century. In the 1970s, writer Charles Bukowski made a nice second income handicapping the horses, and wrote poems about the place. A less happy bit of Santa Anita lore is its use as a holding area for Japanese-Americans on their way to inland internment camps in 1942. Races run in the winter and spring.

285 W Huntington Drive, Arcadia, 91007
Tel: 626 574 7223

THE VENICE ROOM

A marvelous relic of Italian-American San Gabriel Valley cultural life (since 1956), the bar and grill is still run in hands-on fashion by the founding Lombardo family. "Papa" Joe Lombardo's aesthetic vision abides and its worth celebrating: gorgeous pink and blue neon roof sign, trompe l'oeil murals of Venetian canal scenes, cosy deep-cushioned booths and art nouveau foiled wallpaper. The regulars are welcoming to first time visitors, so come in to grill your own 13 oz. steak (baked potato, salad and roll included) or trill a bit of karaoke. Don't miss the vintage photos on display by the bathrooms.

2428 S Garfield Ave., Monterey Park, 91755
Tel: 323 722 3075
Sun-Wed: 8am-12midnight; Thu-Sat: 8am-1am

WORKMAN AND TEMPLE FAMILY HOMESTEAD MUSEUM

A remarkable collection of early California buildings nestled in a most unlikely setting: the middle of a featureless industrial park. But it's Industry (the city of that name, and the income from its namesake) that preserves and maintains the site. Here you'll find the adobe home of pioneer settler William Workman (1842), the private El Campo Santo cemetery (c. 1855) containing the remains of Pio Pico, the last Mexican governor of California, and a gorgeous Spanish Colonial Revival mansion (1922-27) constructed after Workman's grandson Walter Temple struck oil. There's also a pleasant park with a large koi and lily pond. Occasional cultural festivals are held on the grounds, and entry to the historic houses is always free.

15415 E Don Julian Road, City of Industry, 91745
Tel: 626 968 8492 or 626 968 8493
Tours available

South Bay

SOUTH BAY

CHIPS RESTAURANT

A Hawthorne landmark since 1957. The Googie-style diner's most revered feature is the exuberant white script roof signage pinned to green steel mesh panels. Inside, you'll find the classic mid-century casual dining experience: long counter, tuck'n'roll booths, big windows and a menu that's branched out to include Mexican standards, beer and wine. Beach Boys fans making a pilgrimage to the freeway overpass that took out their childhood home will want to stop in for a burger and fries.

11908 Hawthorne Boulevard, Hawthorne, 90250
Tel: 310 679 2947
Daily: 6am-8pm

CHOWDER BARGE

We have Hollywood to thank for this improbably charming portside joint: the craft first hit the water as crew accommodations for the film Mutiny on the Bounty (1935). Now firmly anchored in sleepy Leeward Marina, the city's only floating bar and restaurant seems like the kind of place Jim Rockford would unwind after chasing 1970s bad guys all day. The price is right for fried fish and clam platters, New England style chowder with fried clam strips on top, burgers and beers.

Leeward Bay Marina, 611 Henry Ford Ave., Wilmington, 90744 / Tel: 310 830 7937
Mon: 11am-8pm; Tue: 11am-3pm;
Wed-Thu: 11am-8pm; Fri-Sun: 9am-8pm

© Tony Hoffarth

68   HOW TO FIND OLD LOS ANGELES

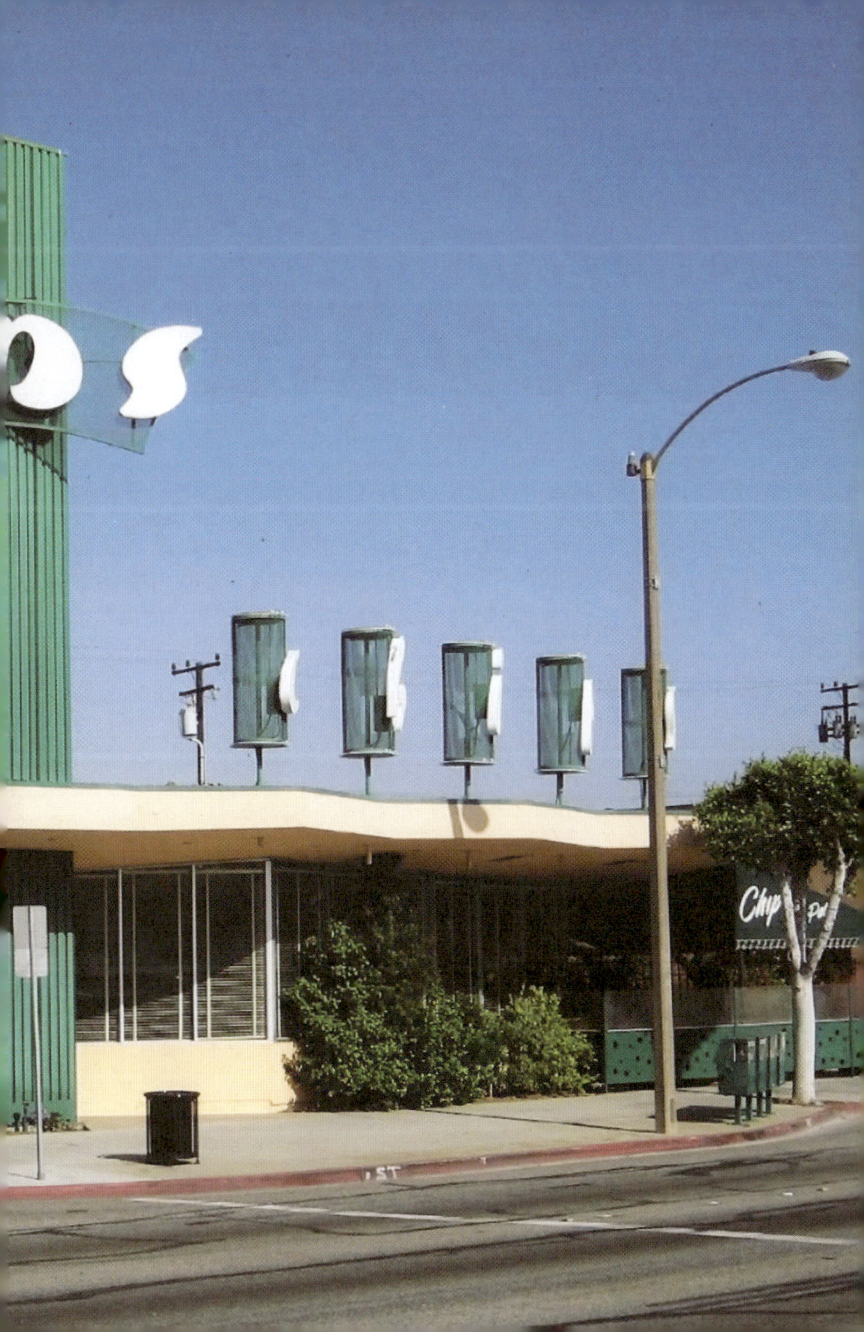
Chip

SOUTH BAY

DOMINGUEZ RANCHO ADOBE

Spanish soldier Juan José Domínguez was a member of the Portolà expedition. For his service to the crown, he received the 75,000 acre Rancho San Pedro land grant. In 1826, his grand-nephew Manuel built a large U-shaped adobe home on the Rancho, which survives as a museum illustrating life during the Californio and early American eras. There is also a wonderful display about early aviators and the Los Angeles International Air Meet held at Dominguez Field (1910). Behind the adobe is a small grotto created by the Claretian Missionaries whose retirement home is on the grounds.

....

18127 S Alameda St., Compton, 90220
Tel: 310 603 0088
Tours available

HOT 'N TOT

Plenty of Angelenos couldn't find Lomita on the map, but at least one thing is worth seeking out: the Hot 'n Tot, a classic booth and counter diner that's been serving the community since 1946. With a fine neon sign and vintage soap box derby tyke pics on view, Hot 'n Tot embraces its history. For the full 1960s aerospace worker experience, there's biscuits and gravy and all the traditional fried breakfast fixings.

....

2347 Pacific Coast Highway, Lomita, 90717
Te: 310 326 9626
Sat-Thu: 6am-9pm; Fri: 5.30am-9pm

JONGEWAARD'S BAKE N BROIL

A favourite in the upscale Bixby Knolls section of Long Beach since 1965, this always-busy family-run comfort food spot takes its baked goods seriously. Spread over several rooms with a homey atmosphere, Jongewaard's has a full American menu including chicken pot pie, but everybody comes in for the mile-high cakes, muffins and flakey pies. For quicker service, snag one of the coveted counter seats.

....

3697 Atlantic Ave., Long Beach, 90807
Tel: 562 595 0396
Mon-Fri: 6.30am-9pm; Sat: 7am-9pm;
Sun: 7am-8.30pm

TONY'S ON THE PIER

Fisherman Tony Trutanich opened his Redondo Beach Pier seafood restaurant in 1952, and while the horseshoe pier has never recovered from the one-two punch of the 1970s-era loss of Redondo's downtown to redevelopment and the huge 1988 fire, "Old" Tony's always satisfies with sunset views, nautical decor, rich clam chowder and gracious servers. Ascend to the Top o' Tony's Bar to enjoy a Fire Chief, a supercharged Mai Tai thats the signature cocktail; you get to keep the logo glass.

....

210 Fisherman's Wharf, Redondo Beach, 90277
Tel: 310 374 1442
Sun-Thu: 11.30am-12midnight;
Fri-Sat: 11.30am-1.30am

South Los Angeles County

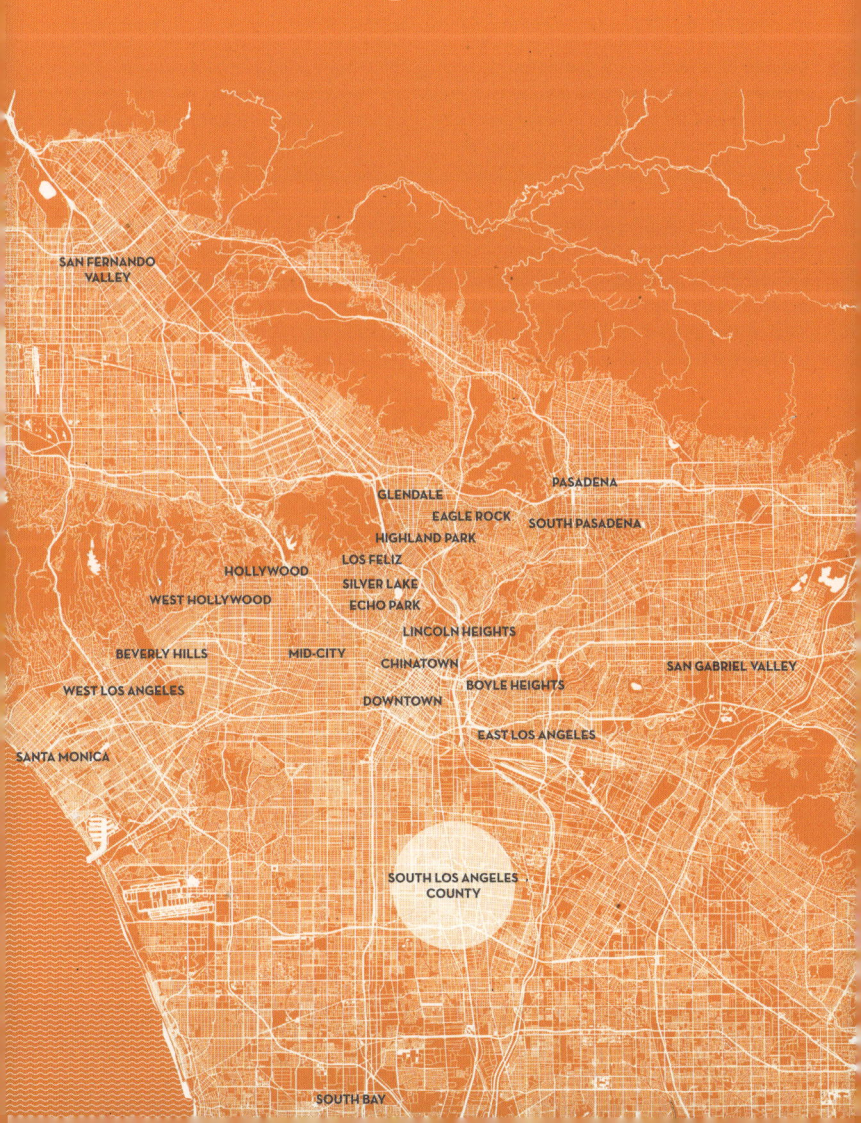

SOUTH LOS ANGELES COUNTY

ART'S CHILI DOG STAND

When the 1992 Rodney King riots broke out, the intersection of Florence and Normandie became notorious for an explosion of violence. But to fans of street cuisine, the corner was already famous as a place of gustatory delight, the home of prickly Art Elkind's counter service shack and his famous chili cheese dog. Art died in 1990, but very little has changed: you still order from the cook, who slips your locally-made all-meat dog into a steamed bun, slaps some mustard on, and tops it with a generous ladle of chili hot from the pot and a cheesy garnish. A South Central original.

1410 W Florence Ave., 90047 / Tel: 323 750 1313
Tue-Sat: 10am-5.30pm

BELLFLOWER BAGELS

One of our favourite examples of adaptive reuse is the transformation of the Bellflower branch of the 1950s-era Big Donut chain into a bagel and coffee stand, with hot, fresh bagels made on site. To make the switch, the huge donut-shaped programmatic lollipop sign has been re-painted with the business name and a delicate pink centre, evoking a schmear of lox spread. The menu includes a selection of donuts for the traditionalists.

17025 Bellflower Boulevard, Bellflower, 90706 / Tel: 562 866 8672
Mon-Sat: 5.30am-7pm; Sun: 7.30am-2pm

CHRIS & PITTS

Chris Pelonis and Morris Pittman launched their Southern California barbeque empire in 1940, in a former dry cleaner's in Lynwood. Today, of three surviving Chris & Pitts restaurants still owned by Chris, this branch retains its daffy 1949 charm. The building pretends to be a rustic log cabin, but the wood is rendered in cartoonish painted swirls and illuminated by an explosive mix of neon and incandescent lights. Inside, locals feast on pit-smoked meats in signature sweet sauce, served with all the fixings. Prices are nice and solo diners can grab a seat at the counter.

9839 Artesia Boulevard, Bellflower, 90706
Tel: 562 867 9160
Tue-Sun: 11am-10pm

CLARKE ESTATE

Los Angeles is ground zero for influential residential architecture, the Hollywood and Westside landscape dotted with houses by Schindler, Neutra, Wright and Eames. But to truly experience the explosion of consciousness that California modernism represents, trek out to industrial Santa Fe Springs. Built in the middle of nowhere in 1919 for a mining millionaire and his bride, Irving Gill's gleaming concrete cube was designed to provide a machine for modern living, free from dusty Victorian nooks and crannies. The heart of the house is a Roman courtyard with incised Mayan details. Corners are rounded for ease of housekeeping, while rooftop patios bring the outdoors in. The effect is stunning and like nothing that came before. But oil well fires soon poisoned the neighbourhood, the Clarkes abandoned ship and Gill's wonderful house was trapped in amber. Six decades later, the city picked it up cheap. It's now a popular wedding venue.

10211 Pioneer Boulevard, Santa Fe Springs, 91905
Tel: 562 863 4896 / 562 868 3876
Tue, Fri & first Sunday of the month: 11am-2pm

GAGE BOWL

For decades, the great American bowling alley was all things to all people: tavern, children care facility, restaurant, social club, gym, dating service. But as the sport fell out of favour in the 1980s and land became more valuable, the giant compounds with their massive surface parking lots were often lost. So it's remarkable to find a full service bowling alley as intact, and beloved by its community, as Huntington Park's Gage Bowl. The alleys thrum with the sound of strikes, while over in the game room, little kids whop their mamas at air hockey and dream of graduating to the pool tables. You can get a greasy meal in the glass-walled diner, or make a new friend at the bar. Gage Bowl is open all day, but you'll want to time your visit to admire the restored boomerang font neon blade sign in all its glory.

3477 E Gage Ave., Huntington Park, 90255
Tel: 323 587 3211
Daily: 24 hours

SOUTH LOS ANGELES COUNTY

HARVEY'S BROILER (BOB'S BIG BOY)

Harvey and Minnie Ortner were a couple on a mission: scout the perfect location for the greatest roadside diner Downey had ever seen. They found it in a chicken farm on a gently curving stretch of Firestone Boulevard. Here, working with architect Paul B. Clayton, they erected a cathedral to the American hamburger, with gleaming neon script and soaring shade structures beneath which roller skating waitresses moved like shooting stars. From 1958 until 2001, Harvey's (later Johnie's) Broiler was the home of Los Angeles County car cruising culture. The restaurant closed and in 2007 the auto dealer tenant began illegal demolition. Public outcry halted the destruction, and a coalition of preservationists and city leaders found an investor willing to rebuild to the original specs. Now a Bob's Big Boy, it's an unlikely historic preservation success story. The hot rods still come every Wednesday night.

7447 Firestone Boulevard, Downey, 90241
Tel: 562 928 2627
Sun-Thu: 7am-11pm; Fri-Sat: 7am-12midnight

MCDONALD'S

A rare surviving example of a Stanley Meston-designed "golden arches" framed food stand (1953) with a vintage animated Speedee character mascot neon sign (1959), this was the third McDonald's restaurant and is the oldest still in

74   HOW TO FIND OLD LOS ANGELES

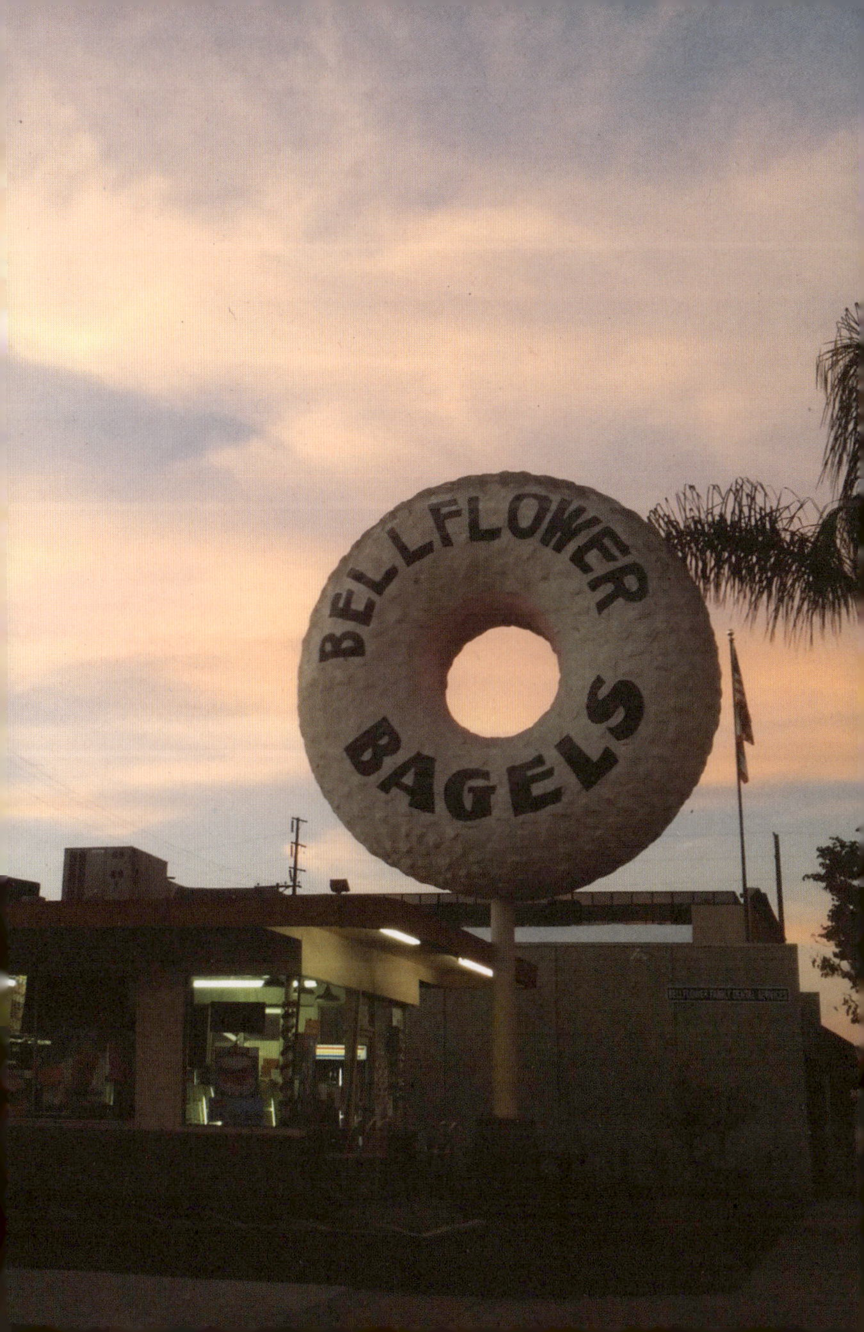
BELLFLOWER
BAGELS

existence. But it's no dusty relic. Carefully sited at one of the busiest intersections in the county, and preserved due to a fluke in the franchise contract, it continues to do a bustling business. Next door is a tiny but packed museum of McDonald's history housed in a replica of the original San Bernardino stand.

.....

10207 LAKEWOOD BOULEVARD, DOWNEY, 90241
DAILY: 8AM-9PM

STOX RESTAURANT & BAKERY

We dig STOX for its attention-seeking vintage sign, with its bold Blackletter "S" and swashbuckling "X," and for its steadfast dedication to serving breakfast (eggs, hotcakes, grilled panini sandwiches) all day long. Since 1954 (at this location since 1962), STOX has been a favourite of Downey folk seeking hearty home cooking and just-baked pies, followed by a shot of something stronger in the attached bar. Try the pineapple upside down muffin.

.....

9518 IMPERIAL HIGHWAY, DOWNEY, 90242
TEL: 562 803 4004
MON-SAT: 6AM-9PM; SUN: 7AM-9PM

TAL'S CAFE

How is it possible for a streamline moderne corner coffee shop with a jazzy red and white neon blade sign to survive, unchanged, in the city that tears itself down for a living? But Tal's is the real McCoy, opened by Herb Stove in 1941, and largely unchanged. Brave the breakfast rush to snag one of five coveted booths, or a counter stool, and pick your poison: a stack of pancakes overlapping the plate, fried chicken and waffles, corned beef hash with home fried potatoes, eggs and grits, or oatmeal if you're slimming. Admire the deep green linoleum tiles, sassy signage, the colourful clientele and the artist behind the grill. This time capsule is cash only.

.....

2701 W FLORENCE AVE., 90043
TEL: 323 751 9749
DAILY: 7AM-3PM

WATTS TOWERS

Acknowledged as one of the world's great folk art environments, Italian immigrant Simon Rodia's spidery openwork towers (1921-1954) soar as high as 99 feet on the narrow plot of land alongside his one-time home. Rodia collected scrap metal and bits of broken tile, mirrors and glass bottles to create his weird garden. After the aged artist walked away from his completed project, the city tried to pull the "dangerous" structures down, only to find they were too strong to tumble under normal demolition standards. A preservation group coalesced around the site, which became a city-owned landmark. Today, an arts centre thrives in the shadows of Rodia's masterpiece, and the public can take a guided tour that points out hidden symbols and technical accomplishments, or marvel from outside the fence.

.....

1727 E 107TH ST., 90002 / TEL: 213 847 4646
TOURS AVAILABLE

West Hollywood

WEST HOLLYWOOD

BARNEY'S BEANERY

The original Beanery, opened in 1927, was a funky roadside beer and onion soup shack, decorated with old license plates. But Barney's big personality and the inspired location, a natural pit stop between Downtown and the coast and an easy drive from the mansions of Beverly Hills, brought the eclectic clientele that secured the joint's legend. By the 1950s, extra rooms were added to accommodate the crowds. Barney is gone now and so is Route 66, but you can still rip it up where most of your Hollywood heroes let their hair down.

8447 SANTA MONICA BOULEVARD,
WEST HOLLYWOOD, 90069 / TEL: 323 654 2287
MON-FRI: 11AM-2AM; SAT-SUN: 9AM-2AM

CARNEY'S

Redevelopment has done a number on the Sunset Strip. But funky Carney's abides. Founded by Pat and John Wolfe in 1975, this classic American burger and hot dog joint is distinguished by its offbeat roadside architecture: you order and dine inside a yellow Union Pacific rail car. Not for the claustrophobic, but it's a fun and affordable relic. Climb aboard for a beer and chili dog with a side of sweet potato fries. For dessert, a chocolate dipped frozen banana on a stick can be enjoyed on the move.

8351 SUNSET BOULEVARD, WEST HOLLYWOOD, 90069
TEL: 323 654 8300
SUN-THU: 11AM-12MIDNIGHT; FRI-SAT: 11AM-3AM

DAN TANA'S

A cosy Italian restaurant with a non-stop bar scene. Owned by Serbian émigré, ex-football player and actor Tana, it is modest and unimposing with red-checked tablecloths and Chianti bottles hanging from the ceiling, but has attracted more than its share of performers since the mid-1960s. The lighting is subdued even if the customers sometimes aren't. Despite the casual atmosphere, it's expensive.

9071 SANTA MONICA BOULEVARD, WEST HOLLYWOOD,
90069 / TEL: 310 275 9444
DAILY: 5PM-1.30AM

GREENBLATT'S FAMOUS DELI

You'll find actors, comics, musicians and locals packing the booths in the tiny two-level dining room, glad of unpretentious fare with its generous proportions, late night hours, free parking, impressive wine shop and somewhat morbid Hollywood literary pedigree. Because the last thing that F. Scott Fitzgerald, staying around the corner at his girlfriend Barbara Graham's apartment in 1940, ever purchased was a Hershey bar from Greenblatt's. He ate it, leaned against Barbara's mantle, and died of a massive coronary. So maybe nix the Double Chocolate Fudge Cake, but the New York Cheesecake is terrific.

8017 SUNSET BOULEVARD, WEST HOLLYWOOD, 90046
TEL: 323 656 0606
DAILY: 10AM-2AM

Westside and beaches

WESTSIDE AND BEACHES

THE APPLE PAN

Arguably the West Side's best burger — hickory-flavoured, placed atop pickles and lettuce with or without a slice of Tillamook cheese (sautéed onions on request) — and a paper plate of French fries with a shaken glob of ketchup, have been plunked down in front of customers since 1947. As have the fine egg salad, and ham and cheese sandwiches. There's a nice variety of pies on offer, including, of course, apple. There are just 26 stools around the horseshoe-shaped counter but even so, prospective diners at key hours should have only a short wait due to the quick speedy service.

10801 WEST PICO BOULEVARD, 90064
TEL: 310 475 3585
TUE-THU: 11AM-12MIDNIGHT; FRI-SAT: 11AM-1AM;
SUN: 11AM-12MIDNIGHT

THE ARSENAL

This bar and restaurant opened in 1950 after several previous identities. Restored in 2003 to its present look, customers have three spaces to choose from — an outside patio, an often noisy main room and lounge, or a quieter restaurant room. Happy Hour is a big draw here, as is the bar food of garlic fries, burgers, poutine and other staples. Steaks are a restaurant favourite.

12012 WEST PICO BOULEVARD, 90064
TEL: 310 575 5511
MON-FRI: 5PM-2AM; SAT-SUN: 6PM-2AM

BEVERLYWOOD BAKERY

The city's oldest bakery, since 1946, offering a wide selection traditional Jewish pastries and breads. Generations of Westsiders know that when the signature hot pink paper box is on the table, good noshing isn't far behind. Popular items include black and white cookies, sliced-to-order rye bread, chocolate-dipped Florentine cookies, cinnamon rugelach, chocolate chip danish and braided challah bread. Not Kosher, which means you can get your babka fix on a Saturday. Look for the blue and white striped awning and the jazzy vintage script sign.

9128 W PICO BOULEVARD, 90035
TEL: 310 278 0122
MON-SAT: 6AM-6PM; SUN: 7AM-5PM

CHEZ JAY'S

A bit of funky beat-era beach culture survives in Jay Fiondella's legendary dive (1959), which recently fought off a demolition threat with an historic landmark designation. The name's a winking nod to Sinatra's joint Chez Joey in Pal Joey, and soon enough, Frank, Sammy, Dean and the rest of the Rat Pack were regulars. The British movie colony, astronauts fresh from meetings at Rand Corp., beach bums and screenwriters followed. With its solid surf 'n' turf menu and unlimited unshelled peanuts on the bar (and shells on the floor), wee Jay's secret weapon is hospitality. Colourful Jay and his

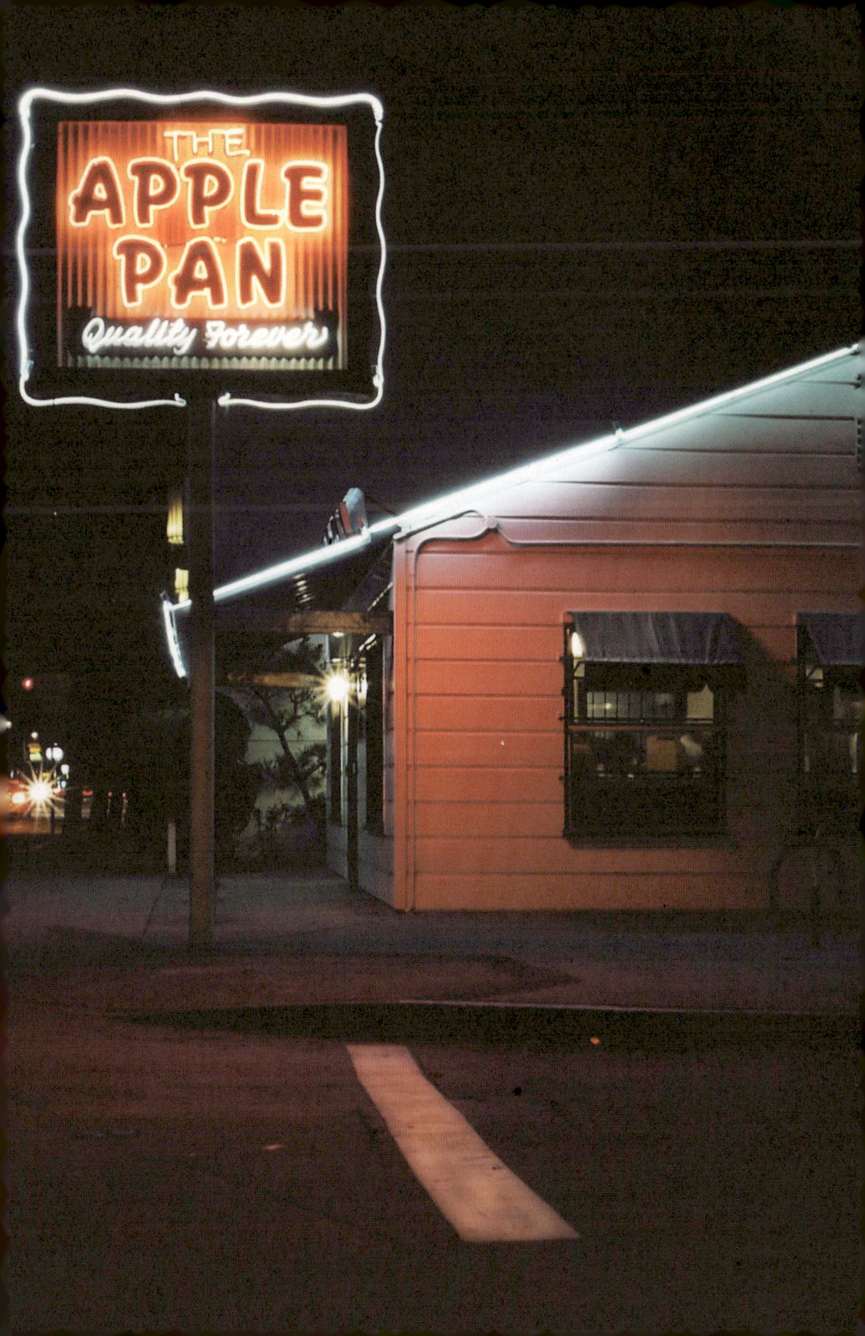
THE
APPLE
PAN
Quality Forever

Ye Olde King's Head

manager mama Alice have left us, but their party is still going strong.

1657 Ocean Ave., Santa Monica, 90401
Tel: 310 395 1741
Mon-Fri: 11.45am-2pm & 5.30pm-9.30pm;
Sat-Sun: 9am-1.45pm & 5.30pm-9.30pm

DINAH'S

Beneath the original sign of the bucket o' chicken since 1959, family-owned and kid-friendly Dinah's diner offers home cooking with the focus on crispy fried chicken infused with secret spices. Signature sides include pineapple coleslaw and banana bread. If you'd got 20 minutes to spare, the baked German apple pancake is a caramelised must for breakfast or a table-shared dessert, and a nice farewell to Los Angeles on your way to LAX. The Dinah's in Glendale has different owners, and is a take-out chicken spot.

6521 Sepulveda Boulevard, 90045
Tel: 310 645 0456
Daily: 6am-10pm

FOUNTAIN COFFEE SHOP AT THE BEVERLY HILLS HOTEL

The glamorous Beverly Hills Hotel, completed in 1912, didn't get its downstairs Fountain Coffee Shop until 1949, but thankfully precious little has been altered since then. A polished curved black counter top with 19 white wrought-iron chairs (fixed to the floor) surrounded by the famous green banana leaf on pale pink wallpaper all remain. This is a refined, platonic ideal of coffee-shop/diner fare. Every plate is lighter, fresher and less greasy than anywhere else and, of course, much more expensive. A lunch for two with tip can edge into $70. But you're in a historic spot waited on by friendly, attentive staff, with made-on-the-premises food and sterling service — all of which does a lot to offset any pecuniary damage.

9641 West Sunset Boulevard, 90210
Tel: 310 276 2251
Daily: 7am-7pm

THE GALLEY

When Raymond Chandler wrote about Santa Monica, he called it Bay City and marveled at how bone-deep crooked one little seaside town could be. That rough noir place is long gone, replaced by yoga studios and juice bars. And yet the Galley (1934) survives, this neon-decked, nautical-themed, evenings-only Main Street joint, like a time traveler with a bit of an attitude. The walls are thick with Hollywood memorabilia (including set pieces from Mutiny On The Bounty), the Christmas lights twinkle all year round, and you'll be dining or imbibing among dusty nets and blowfish lanterns. Tuck one of the leggy lady captain cocktail napkins in your pocket as a keepsake.

2442 Main St., Santa Monica, 90405
Tel: 310 452 1934
Mon-Sat: 5pm-11pm; Sun: 1pm-11pm

WESTSIDE AND BEACHES

KRAMER'S PIPE & TOBACCO SHOP

Should you subscribe to that most 20th century of vices, why not indulge your tobacco lust at one of the last family-owned Beverly Hills retail shops? The proudly retro Kramer's (since 1949) is a miniature museum of vintage smoking ephemera, with a large stock of cigars, pipes, lighters and cigarettes by the pack displayed in the vintage wooden cases that founder Al Kramer designed and built. But it's the custom tobacco blends that made Kramer's name. Take a pouch of Danny Kaye's or Cary Grant's personal pipe mix home for the complete Old Hollywood experience.

9531 SANTA MONICA BOULEVARD, BEVERLY HILLS, 90210 / TEL: 310 273 9777
TUE-SAT: 11AM-6PM

LAWRY'S THE PRIME RIB

In mid-century, Los Angeles foodie culture had an undeniable home: Restaurant Row (La Cienega Boulevard from Beverly to Sunset). Here was found the hearty Continental fare and seamless hospitality that drew upscale crowds away from Sunset Strip nightclubs. The Bantam Cock, Richlor's and Tail o' the Cock are distant memories, but Lawry's, which has never messed with its formula, survives and thrives. Regulars go for the juicy prime rib served from the rolling cart, with traditional sides like buttery mashed potatoes, creamed spinach, Yorkshire pudding and an extra dollop of creamy horseradish. It's an old fashioned, grown-up kind of place that's still earning young fans. Pricey and a bit stuffy, reservations are a must.

100 N LA CIENEGA BOULEVARD, BEVERLY HILLS, 90211 / TEL: 310 652 2827
MON-FRI: 5PM-9.30PM; SAT: 4PM-10PM; SUN: 4PM-9PM

PANN'S COFFEE SHOP

For homesick Angelenos flying into LAX, this is a nearby full-strength shot of late-1950s coffee-shop nirvana by quintessential Googie architects Armet & Davis. A hot neon sign on a pylon shoots through a cantilevered roof that dips over the glass-surrounded interior. The slightly sunken dining area — patterned Formica, rough stone walls, long counter and roomy leatherette booths — looks out over the night-lit tropical vegetation. All this and a great patty melt — the definite yardstick for surviving coffee shops. Ask if their famous, but infrequent, corned-beef hash is being served.

6710 LATIJERA BOULEVARD, 90045
TEL: 323 776 3770
SUN-WED: 7AM-9PM; THU-SAT: 7AM-10PM

RANDY'S DONUTS

One of the most photographed buildings in Los Angeles due to its proximity to LAX and the fact that it has a huge donut on the roof, Randy's opened in 1953 as the

Fountain Coffee Shop at the Beverly Hills Hotel

second branch of the Big Donut drive-in chain. Architect Henry J. Goodwin designed the moderne storefront as a sturdy platform for the steel and concrete pastry logo-sign, an astonishing 32 feet in diameter. It doesn't matter what time your flight leaves; Randy's never closes. Try the apple fritters.

805 W Manchester Boulevard, Inglewood, 90301
Tel: 310 645 4707
Daily: 24 hours

REEL INN

We had to include at least one Pacific Coast Highway beach-bum shack. The rough wood building with outdoor deck and tables has gone through several owners and identities since 1947. Starting as a Mexican restaurant, it became The Raft from the mid-1960s to mid-1970s, when it was a favourite of surfers as well as Lee Marvin and other hard-boiled Hollywood thesps. Fresh broiled fish and shellfish (on plates or in tacos) along with soups, salads and sides are listed on blackboards above the ordering window to be eaten inside or out.

18661 Pacific Coast Highway, Malibu, 90265
Tel: 310 456 8221
Daily: 11am-9pm

SANTA MONICA PIER CAROUSEL

Not long after the Santa Monica Pier opened in 1909, plans were underway to add an Amusement Park. By 1916 the Hippodrome building was built to house the carousel, and both have survived to become Santa Monica's first official historic landmark. The pier got a new amusement park in the 1990s and, recently, what is reported to be a decent hamburger stand, but we suggest you opt instead for a ride on one of those old revolving merry-go-round horses for $2 (kids $1).

200 Santa Monica Pier, #A, 90401
Tel: 310 394 8042
Thu-Mon: from 11am
Closing times vary, so best to call ahead

SELF-REALIZATION FELLOWSHIP LAKE SHRINE TEMPLE

The history of Los Angeles is that of esoteric religious movements, among them SRF, founded by Paramahansa Yogananda in 1920 with the aim of bringing yoga to the West. In the 1940s, Yogananda acquired this remarkable property, a spring-fed lake with a fairytale windmill, tucked into a canyon steps from the sea. Flowers were planted, paths developed and a memorial to world peace installed, containing some of Gandhi's ashes. Since 1950, the site has been open to the public as a shrine of all religions, a secret garden alive with swans, turtles and dragonflies. Elvis Presley, a noted seeker, loved the place.

17190 Sunset Boulevard, Pacific Palisades, 90272 / Tel: 310 454 4114
Tue-Sat: 9am-4.30pm; Sun: 12noon-4.30pm

SERRA SPRINGS

On the campus of University High School in West Los Angeles is one of the city's most ancient landmarks: Serra Springs, twin natural pools that produce more than 20,000 gallons of fresh water each day. The native Tongva people considered the water source sacred, and called it "Kuruvungna" ("a place where we are in the sun"), also the name of the nearby village. The springs were observed by members of Portolá's 1769 expedition, and given their Spanish name in recognition of Franciscan Father Serra having said mass there. When the school was built in 1924, the springs were incorporated into the landscaping. Today, the largest spring is overseen by the Gabrielino/Tongva Springs Foundation, a native group that leads tours, maintains traditional plantings and a museum of artifacts uncovered on the site, and advocates the preservation of the springs and aquifer.

1439 S BARRINGTON AVE., 90025
TEL: 310 8062418
FIRST SAT OF THE MONTH: 10AM-3PM

TITO'S TACOS

This famed Culver City joint (since 1959) with the perpetual line to the curb serves "Mexican" food, an unashamedly gringo spin on the cuisine of our near neighbour. Whether you choose to take out or eat in the no-frills dining room, odds are you'll be ordering hard shell tacos laden with ground beef, iceberg lettuce and an ocean of shredded yellow cheese, served in a thin cardboard box. The shell will collapse after the first bite, coating your hands in oily red sauce, and you'll scrape the innards up with tortilla chips. If you grew up on Tito's, the experience will scratch a deep nostalgic itch. If you grew up eating real Mexican food, the Tito's scene is an only-in-L.A. culinary experience worth having, once.

11222 WASHINGTON PLACE, CULVER CITY, 90230
TEL: 310 391 5780
SUN-THU: 10AM-10PM; FRI-SAT: 10AM-11PM

WILL ROGERS STATE HISTORIC PARK

Will Rogers was one of Hollywood's first superstars, a charming vaudevillian cowboy who branched out into every form of mass media available. His retreat was this sprawling ranch in Pacific Palisades, containing a rustic 31-room mansion, polo fields and hiking trails. Rogers died in a plane crash in 1935, and in 1944 the state accepted his family's gift of the property. Visitors can hike through the native chaparral forest to the stunning Inspiration Point, picnic on the lawns, shop for books about Rogers in the Visitors Center or learn to ride horses in the old corral. The house, still filled with personal memorabilia and vintage Western furnishings, is open for free tours throughout the week.

1501 WILL ROGERS STATE PARK ROAD, PACIFIC PALISADES, 90272

WESTSIDE AND BEACHES

Tel: 310 454 8212
Park, daily, including holidays
Parking lot: 8am–sunset
Gift Store in visitor centre: Thu–Sun: 10.30am–5.30pm
Ranch House tours: Thu–Fri: 11am–3pm hourly; Sat–Sun: 10am–4pm hourly

YE OLDE KING'S HEAD

Santa Monica is the closest thing L.A. has to a Little UK district, and since Phil and Ruth Elwell set up shop in 1974, Southland Brits have been soothing their homesickness at this seaside compound comprised of pub, tea room and import grocery store (for all Christmas cracker and canned mushy pea needs). For the lifted pinkie crowd, finger sandwiches, scones and champagne is served on fancy china in a timbered red room lined with portraits of monarchs. The pub is more casual, with memorabilia-coated walls, darts, UK sporting events on the telly, a full kitchen serving the range of pub grub, and a colourful expat clientele. Come count down the new year at 4pm local time next December 31.

116 Santa Monica Boulevard, Santa Monica, 90401
Tel: 310 451 1402
Restaurant: Mon–Wed: 9am–10pm; Thu: 9am–11pm; Fri: 9am–12midnight; Sat: 8am–12midnight; Sun: 8am–11pm
Pub: Daily: 10am–2am
Store: Sun–Thu: 10am–8pm; Fri–Sat: 10am–10pm

Santa Monica Pier Carousel
© Dan Gaken

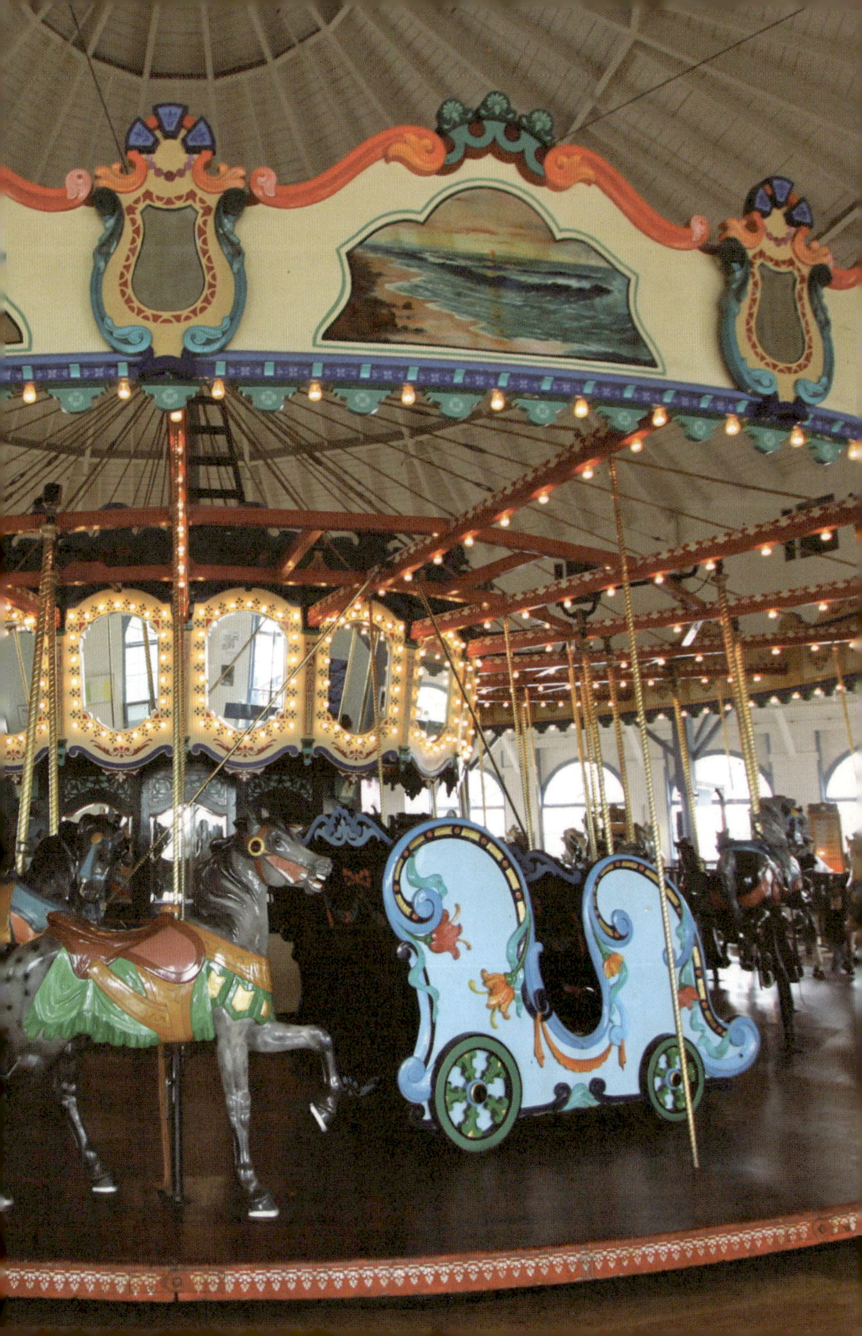

BAR

Union Station

INDEX

EATING AND DRINKING
101 Coffee Shop **36**
Al & Bea's **20**
Apple Pan, The **80**
Arsenal, The **80**
Art's Chili Dog Stand **72**
Astro Family Restaurant **22**
Barney's Beanery **78**
Bear Pit Bar-B-Q, The **54**
Bellflower Bagels **72**
Beverlywood Bakery **80**
Biltmore Hotel **8**
Boardner's Bar **36**
Bun 'n Burger **58**
Canter's Deli **78**
Carney's **36**
Casa Bianca **30**
Chez Jay's **80**
Chips Restaurant **68**
Chowder Barge **68**
Chris & Pitts **72**
Cicada Club Restaurant **10**
Clearman's Steak 'n Stein **58**
Clifton's Cafeteria **10**
Cole's **11**
Dal Rae, The **60**
Dan Tana's **78**
Derby Restaurant, The **60**
Dinah's **83**
Donut Hole, The **62**
Dresden Room **22**
Eastside Market & Italian Deli **11**
El Cholo **48**
El Cid **22**
El Coyote Café **36**
Embers Lounge, The **62**
Fair Oaks Pharmacy and Soda Fountain **30**
Formosa Café **37**
Fosselman's **62**
Fountain Coffee Shop at the Beverly Hills Hotel **83**
Galley, The **83**
Gilmore Gas (Starbucks Coffee Shop) **37**
Grand Central Market **11**
Greenblatt's Famous Deli **78**
Gus's Barbecue **32**
H.M.S. Bounty **48**
Harvey's Broiler (Bob's Big Boy) **74**
Hat, The **64**
Hop Louie **12**
Hot 'n Tot **70**
House of Pies **25**
Idle Hour, The **46**
Jongewaard's Bake n Broil **70**
La Golondrina Mexican Café **12**
Langer's Deli **49**
Lanza Brothers Market **12**
Lawry's The Prime Rib **84**
Magic Castle, The **41**
Manuel's Original El Tepeyac Café **20**
Mary's Market & Canyon Café **64**
McDonald's **74**
Miceli's **41**
Moun of Tunis **41**
Musso & Frank Grill **41**
Nick's Coffee Shop **50**
Norms La Cienega **41**
Original Farmer's Market, The **37**
Original Pantry Café **17**
Original Tommy's Hamburgers **50**
Otomisan **20**
Pacific Dining Car **50**
Pann's Coffee Shop **84**
Papa Cristo's **51**
Philippe The Original **17**
Phoenix Bakery **17**
Pie 'n Burger **34**
Pink's Hot Dogs **51**
Pioneer Chicken **20**
Prince, The **52**
Randy's Donuts **84**
Red Lion Tavern **27**
Reel Inn **86**
Rod's Grill **65**
San Antonio Winery **18**
Smoke House, The **56**
STOX Restaurant & Bakery **76**
Taix **27**
Tal's Cafe **76**
Tally Rand **56**
Tam O'Shanter **27**
Taylor's Steakhouse **52**
Tiki-Ti **28**
Tito's Tacos **87**
Tom Bergin's Public House **52**
Tony's on the Pier **70**
Venice Room, The **66**
Ye Olde King's Head **88**

SHOPPING
Broguiere's Farm Fresh Dairy **58**
Caravan Book Store **10**
Divine's Furniture **60**
Eastside Market & Italian Deli **11**
Grand Central Market **11**
Kramer's Pipe & Tobacco Shop **84**
Lanza Brothers Market **12**
Larry Edmunds Bookshop **38**
Macy's (formerly Bullock's Department Store) **34**
Oceanic Arts **65**
San Antonio Winery **18**

THINGS TO SEE AND DO
Alvarado Terrace **46**
Angels Flight Railway **8**
Bob Baker Marionette Theater **46**
Bradbury Building **8**
Brand Library & Art Center **30**
Broadway Theater District **8**
Carroll Avenue **22**
Clarke Estate **72**

HOW TO FIND OLD LOS ANGELES

INDEX

Confluence of the L.A. River and Arroyo Seco **11**
Dominguez Rancho Adobe **70**
Forest Lawn Cemetery **32**
Gage Bowl **73**
Grandma Prisbrey's Bottle Village **54**
Grauman's Chinese Theatre **38**
Grauman's Egyptian Theatre **38**
Griffith Park Observatory **24**
Heritage Square **24**
Hollyhock House **25**
Hollywood Forever Cemetery **38**
Huntington Desert Garden **32**
Judson Studios **26**
La Brea Tar Pits **49**
Lasky-DeMille Barn **41**
Los Angeles City Hall **14**
Los Angeles County Arboretum and Botanic Garden **64**
Los Angeles Public Library **14**
Lummis House **14**
Magic Castle, The **41**
Natural History Museum & Exposition Park Rose Garden **49**
Pasadena US Post Office **34**
Plaza, The **18**
Santa Anita Park **66**
Santa Monica Pier Carousel **86**
Self-Realization Fellowship Lake Shrine Temple **86**
Serra Springs **87**
Sister Aimee's Parsonage **27**
Travel Town **28**
Union Station **18**
Vedanta Society of Southern California **44**
Vista Theatre **28**
Wattles Park **44**
Watts Towers **76**
Will Rogers State Historic Park **87**
Workman and Temple Family Homestead Museum **66**

INDEX

INDEX TWO
A-Z listing by name and subject

101 Coffee Shop **36**
24 HOURS (OPENING)
   Astro Family Restaurant **22**
   Canter's Deli **78**
   Gage Bowl **73**
   Original Pantry Café **17**
   Original Tommy's Hamburgers **50**
   Pacific Dining Car **50**
   Randy's Donuts **84**
   Union Station **18**
48 HOURS (FILM)
   Gilmore Gas (Starbucks Coffee Shop) **37**
AIR HOCKEY
   Gage Bowl **73**
Al & Bea's **20**
ALDOUS HUXLEY
   Vedanta Society of Southern California **44**
Alvarado Terrace **46**
AMBASSADOR HOTEL
   H.M.S. Bounty **48**
Angels Flight Railway **8**
ANIMALS
   La Brea Tar Pits **49**
ANTIQUES
   Divine's Furniture **60**
APPLE FRITTERS
   Randy's Donuts **84**
Apple Pan, The **80**
ARCHITECTURE
   Astro Family Restaurant **22**
   Bradbury Building **8**
   Carroll Avenue **22**
   Carney's **36**
   Clarke Estate **72**
   Los Angeles City Hall **14**
   Los Angeles Public Library **14**
   McDonald's **74**
   Norms La Cienega **41**
   Union Station **18**
   Watts Towers **76**
ARMET & DAVIS
   Astro Family Restaurant **22**
   Norms La Cienega **41**
   Pann's Coffee Shop **84**
Arsenal, The **80**
ART
   Brand Library & Art Center **30**
ART DECO
   Cicada Club Restaurant **10**
   Gilmore Gas (Starbucks Coffee Shop) **37**
   Los Angeles Public Library **14**
   Macy's (formerly Bullock's Department Store) **34**
   Union Station **18**
ART STUDIO
   Judson Studios **26**
Art's Chili Dog Stand **72**
ARTS CENTRE
   Watts Towers **76**
ASHRAM
   Vedanta Society of Southern California **44**
Astro Family Restaurant **22**
ASTRONAUTS
   Chez Jay's **80**
ATRIUM
   Los Angeles Public Library **14**
BABY DOLLS
   Grandma Prisbrey's Bottle Village **54**
BAGELS
   Bellflower Bagels **72**
BAKERY
   Beverlywood Bakery **80**
   Canter's Deli **78**
   Jongewaard's Bake n Broil **70**
   Phoenix Bakery **17**
   STOX Restaurant & Bakery **76**
BANANA SPLIT
   Fosselman's **62**

BAR
   Biltmore Hotel **8**
   Cicada Club Restaurant **10**
   Cole's **11**
   Dan Tana's **78**
   Gage Bowl **73**
   Hop Louie **12**
   STOX Restaurant & Bakery **76**
   Venice Room, The **66**
BARBECUE
   Bear Pit Bar-B-Q, The **54**
   Chris & Pitts **72**
   Gus's Barbecue **32**
Barber shop
   Macy's (formerly Bullock's Department Store) **34**
Barney's Beanery **78**
BATHROOM
   Sister Aimee's Parsonage **27**
BEACH
   Reel Inn **86**
BEACH BOYS
   Chips Restaurant **68**
   Prince, The **52**
BEACH BUMS
   Chez Jay's **80**
Bear Pit Bar-B-Q, The **54**
BEAUX ARTS
   Pasadena US Post Office **34**
BEER
   Chips Restaurant **68**
   Idle Hour, The **54**
BELLY DANCERS
   Moun of Tunis **41**
Beverlywood Bakery **80**
BICARBONATE OF SODA
   Pink's Hot Dogs **51**
Biltmore Hotel **8**
BIRD-WATCHING
   Chowder Barge **68**
BISTRO
   Taix **27**
BISCUITS AND GRAVY
   Hot 'n Tot **70**

HOW TO FIND OLD LOS ANGELES

INDEX

BLACK DAHLIA, THE
   Boardner's Bar **36**
BLACK EYE MILKSHAKE
   101 Coffee Shop **36**
BLUES
   Gus's Barbecue **32**
Boardner's Bar **36**
Bob Baker Marionette Theater **46**
BOB'S DONUTS
   Original Farmer's Market, The **37**
BOBBY KENNEDY
   H.M.S. Bounty **48**
BOHEMIAN
   Mary's Market & Canyon Café **64**
BOOKSHOP
   Caravan Book Store **10**
   Larry Edmunds Bookshop **38**
   Lasky-DeMille Barn **41**
   Vedanta Society of Southern California **44**
BOOTHS
   Chips Restaurant **68**
   Cole's **11**
   Dresden Room **22**
   Greenblatt's Famous Deli **78**
   Hot 'n Tot **70**
   House of Pies **25**
   Langer's Deli **49**
   Original Pantry Café **17**
   Otomisan **20**
   Pann's Coffee Shop **84**
   Smoke House, The **56**
   Tal's Cafe **76**
   Tally Rand **56**
   Venice Room, The **66**
BOTANIC GARDEN
   Huntington Desert Garden **32**
   Los Angeles County Arboretum and Botanic Garden **64**
BOTTLED SAUCE
   Bear Pit Bar-B-Q, The **54**

BOWLING ALLEY
   Gage Bowl **73**
Bradbury Building **8**
Brand Library & Art Center **30**
BREAKFAST
   Hat, The **64**
   Hot 'n Tot **70**
   Mary's Market & Canyon Café **64**
   Pacific Dining Car **50**
   STOX Restaurant & Bakery **76**
   Tal's Cafe **76**
BRISKET
   Idle Hour, The **54**
BRITISH
   Ye Olde King's Head **88**
Broadway Theater District **8**
Broguiere's Farm Fresh Dairy **58**
BRUNCH
   El Cid **22**
   Smoke House, The **56**
BUGSY SIEGEL
   Formosa Café **37**
Bun 'n Burger **58**
BURGER
   Apple Pan, The **80**
   Arsenal, The **80**
   Bun 'n Burger **58**
   Carney's **36**
   Chips Restaurant **68**
   Harvey's Broiler (Bob's Big Boy) **74**
   McDonald's **74**
   Original Tommy's Hamburgers **50**
   Pie 'n Burger **34**
BURRITO
   Al & Bea's **20**
   Manuel's Original El Tepeyac Café **20**
BUSTY LASSIES
   Embers Lounge, The **62**
BUTCHER
   Grand Central Market **11**

BUTTER
   Derby Restaurant, The **60**
CACTUS
   Huntington Desert Garden **32**
CAFÉ
   Manuel's Original El Tepeyac Café **20**
   Original Pantry Café **17**
   Philippe The Original **17**
CAFETERIA
   Clifton's Cafeteria **10**
   San Antonio Winery **18**
CAKES
   Jongewaard's Bake n Broil **70**
   Phoenix Bakery **17**
CANDY SOUVENIRS
   Fair Oaks Pharmacy and Soda Fountain **30**
Canter's Deli **78**
Caravan Book Store **10**
Carney's **36**
CAROUSEL
   Santa Monica Pier Carousel **86**
Carroll Avenue **22**
Casa Bianca **30**
CBS TELEVISION
   Original Farmer's Market, The **37**
Cecil B. DeMille
   Lasky-DeMille Barn **41**
CEMETERY
   Brand Library & Art Center **30**
   Forest Lawn Cemetery **32**
   Hollywood Forever Cemetery **38**
   Workman and Temple Family Homestead Museum **66**
CHARLES BUKOWSKI
   Boardner's Bar **36**
   House of Pies **25**
   Los Angeles Public Library **14**
   Santa Anita Park **66**
CHARLES MAURICE DE TALLEYRAND

INDEX

Tally Rand 56
CHARLES NELSON REILLY
   El Cid 22
CHARLIE CHAPLIN
   Original Pantry Café 17
Chez Jay's 80
CHIANTI
   Dan Tana's 78
CHICKEN POT PIE
   Jongewaard's Bake n Broil 70
CHILI DOG
   Art's Chili Dog Stand 72
   Original Tommy's Hamburgers 50
CHINESE BAKERY
   Phoenix Bakery 17
CHINESE FOOD
   Formosa Café 37
   Hop Louie 12
Chips Restaurant 68
CHOWDER
   Chowder Barge 68
   Tony's on the Pier 70
Chowder Barge 68
Chris & Pitts 72
CHRISTINE STERLING
   Plaza, The 18
CHRISTOPHER ISHERWOOD
   Vedanta Society of Southern California 44
Cicada Club Restaurant 10
CIGARETTES & CIGARS
   Kramer's Pipe & Tobacco Shop 84
CINEMA
   Grauman's Chinese Theatre 38
   Grauman's Egyptian Theatre 38
   Vista Theatre 28
   Hollywood Forever Cemetery 38
CIRCULAR FIRE PIT
   Clearman's Steak 'n Stein 58
Clarke Estate 72

Clearman's Steak 'n Stein 58
Clifton's Cafeteria 10
COCKTAILS
   Biltmore Hotel 8
   Clifton's Cafeteria 10
   Cole's 11
   Dal Rae, The 60
   Dresden Room 22
   Formosa Café 37
   Galley, The 83
   Hop Louie 12
   Tally Rand 56
   Tiki-Ti 28
   Tony's on the Pier 70
COFFEE
   101 Coffee Shop 36
   Astro Family Restaurant 22
   Bellflower Bagels 72
   Donut Hole, The 62
   Fountain Coffee Shop at the Beverly Hills Hotel 83
   Gilmore Gas (Starbucks Coffee Shop) 37
   Nick's Coffee Shop 50
   Pann's Coffee Shop 84
   Philippe The Original 17
   Tal's Cafe 76
   Tally Rand 56
Cole's 11
COLLECTIONS
   Grandma Prisbrey's Bottle Village 54
COLONEL GRIFFITH J. GRIFFITH
   Griffith Park Observatory 24
COMFORT FOOD
   Bun 'n Burger 58
Confluence of the L.A. River and Arroyo Seco 11
CORNED BEEF HASH
   Pann's Coffee Shop 84
   Tal's Cafe 76
COUNTER
   Chips Restaurant 68
   Chris & Pitts 72

   Hot 'n Tot 70
   Pie 'n Burger 34
   Tally Rand 56
COWBOY
   Will Rogers State Historic Park 87
CRAB
   Musso & Frank Grill 41
CREAM SODA
   Langer's Deli 49
DAIRY
   Broguiere's Farm Fresh Dairy 58
Dal Rae, The 60
Dan Tana's 78
DANCING
   Cicada Club Restaurant 10
   La Golondrina Mexican Café 12
DANNY KAYE
   Kramer's Pipe & Tobacco Shop 84
   Smoke House, The 56
DELI
   Canter's Deli 78
   Eastside Market & Italian Deli 11
   Greenblatt's Famous Deli 78
   Langer's Deli 49
   Lanza Brothers Market 12
DEPARTMENT STORE
   Macy's (formerly Bullock's Department Store) 34
Derby Restaurant, The 60
DESERT
   Huntington Desert Garden 32
Dinah's 83
DINER
   Astro Family Restaurant 22
   Bun 'n Burger 58
   Dinah's 83
   Fountain Coffee Shop at the Beverly Hills Hotel 83
   Gage Bowl 73

HOW TO FIND OLD LOS ANGELES   95

INDEX

Harvey's Broiler (Bob's Big Boy) **74**
Philippe The Original **17**
DIRE WOLF
　La Brea Tar Pits **49**
DISNEY ANIMATION STUDIO
　Tam O'Shanter **27**
DIVE BAR
　Boardner's Bar **36**
　Chez Jay's **80**
　Embers Lounge, The **62**
　Hop Louie **12**
Divine's Furniture **60**
Dominguez Rancho Adobe **70**
DONUTS
　Bellflower Bagels **72**
　Donut Hole, The **62**
　Randy's Donuts **84**
Donut Hole, The **62**
DRAGONFLIES
　Self-Realization Fellowship Lake Shrine Temple **86**
Dresden Room **22**
DU-PAR'S RESTAURANT
　Original Farmer's Market, The **37**
Eames
　Clarke Estate **72**
Eastside Market & Italian Deli **11**
Edward Doheny
　Bob Baker Marionette Theater **46**
EGGNOG
　Broguiere's Farm Fresh Dairy **58**
EGGS
　Mary's Market & Canyon Café **64**
EGYPTIAN
　Grauman's Egyptian Theatre **38**
　Vista Theatre **28**
El Cholo **48**

El Cid **22**
El Coyote Café **36**
ELIZABETH SHORT
　Boardner's Bar **36**
ELVIS PRESLEY
　Self-Realization Fellowship Lake Shrine Temple **86**
Embers Lounge, The **62**
ERROL FLYNN
　Boardner's Bar **36**
ESQUIRE THEATRE
　Canter's Deli **78**
EXCAVATION
　La Brea Tar Pits **49**
EXOTIC
　Oceanic Arts **65**
F. SCOTT FITZGERALD
　Greenblatt's Famous Deli **78**
　Musso & Frank Grill **41**
Fair Oaks Pharmacy and Soda Fountain **30**
FAMILY BUSINESS
　Caravan Book Store **10**
　Divine's Furniture **60**
　Fosselman's **62**
　Nick's Coffee Shop **50**
　Venice Room, The **66**
FANTASY ISLAND
　Los Angeles County Arboretum and Botanic Garden **64**
FARM
　Broguiere's Farm Fresh Dairy **58**
　Original Farmer's Market, The **37**
FAST FOOD
　Art's Chili Dog Stand **72**
　Grand Central Market **11**
　Hat, The **64**
　McDonald's **74**
　Original Tommy's Hamburgers **50**
　Pink's Hot Dogs **51**
　Pioneer Chicken **20**

FETA
　Papa Cristo's **51**
FILM LOCATION
　Bradbury Building **8**
　Carroll Avenue **22**
　Cicada Club Restaurant **10**
　Gilmore Gas (Starbucks Coffee Shop) **37**
　Lasky-DeMille Barn **41**
　Los Angeles City Hall **14**
FILM SCREENINGS
　Hollywood Forever Cemetery **38**
FISH
　Reel Inn **86**
FISHMONGER
　Grand Central Market **11**
FLAMENCO
　El Cid **22**
　Idle Hour, The **54**
FLOATING ESTABLISHMENTS
　Chowder Barge **68**
FOLK ART
　Dominguez Rancho Adobe **70**
　Grandma Prisbrey's Bottle Village **54**
　Watts Towers **76**
Forest Lawn Cemetery **32**
Formosa Café **37**
Fosselman's **62**
FOSSILS
　La Brea Tar Pits **49**
Fountain Coffee Shop at the Beverly Hills Hotel **83**
FRANK HOWARD BOWERS
　Embers Lounge, The **62**
FRANK LLOYD WRIGHT
　Chips Restaurant **68**
　Clarke Estate **72**
　Hollyhock House **25**
FRANK SINATRA
　Chez Jay's **80**
　Dresden Room **22**
　Patsy Pizza **37**

INDEX

FREE PARKING
   Greenblatt's Famous Deli **78**
   Langer's Deli **49**
   Original Pantry Café **17**
FRENCH DIP
   101 Coffee Shop **36**
   Cole's **11**
   Philippe The Original **17**
FRENCH FOOD
   Taix **27**
FRIED CHICKEN
   Dinah's **83**
   Pioneer Chicken **20**
   Tal's Cafe **76**
FURNITURE
   Divine's Furniture **60**
Gage Bowl **73**
GALLERY
   Judson Studios **26**
Galley, The **83**
GARDEN
   Huntington Desert Garden **32**
   Los Angeles County Arboretum and Botanic Garden **64**
   Lummis House **14**
   Natural History Museum & Exposition Park Rose Garden **49**
   Self-Realization Fellowship Lake Shrine Temple **86**
   Vedanta Society of Southern California **44**
   Wattles Park **44**
GARLIC FRIES
   Arsenal, The **80**
GARLIC TOAST
   Smoke House, The **56**
GERALD HEARD
   Vedanta Society of Southern California **44**
GERMAN BEER
   Red Lion Tavern **27**
GIANT BEER BARREL
   Idle Hour, The **54**

GIFT SHOP
   Magic Castle, The **41**
   Will Rogers State Historic Park **87**
Gilmore Gas (Starbucks) **37**
GLASS BOTTLES
   Grandma Prisbrey's Bottle Village **54**
GOLD RUSH
   Griffith Park Observatory **24**
   Los Angeles County Arboretum and Botanic Garden **64**
GOLDEN ARCHES
   McDonald's **74**
GOLD STAR STUDIOS
   Pink's Hot Dogs **51**
GOOD VIBRATIONS
   Prince, The **52**
GOOGIE ARCHITECTURE
   Astro Family Restaurant **22**
   Chips Restaurant **68**
   Norms La Cienega **41**
   Pann's Coffee Shop **84**
   Rod's Grill **65**
GORDON KAUFMANN
   Santa Anita Park **66**
GOSPEL CAR
   Sister Aimee's Parsonage **27**
Grand Central Market **11**
Grandma Prisbrey's Bottle Village **54**
Graüman's Chinese Theatre **38**
Graüman's Egyptian Theatre **38**
GREEK FOOD
   Astro Family Restaurant **22**
   Papa Cristo's **51**
GREEK THEATRE
   Griffith Park Observatory **24**
Greenblatt's Famous Deli **78**
Griffith Park Observatory **24**
GRILL
   Rod's Grill **65**
   Venice Room, The **66**
GROTTO

   Dominguez Rancho Adobe **70**
GUIDED TOUR
   Broadway Theater District **8**
   Grandma Prisbrey's Bottle Village **54**
   Grauman's Egyptian Theatre **38**
   Hollyhock House **25**
   Judson Studios **26**
   Watts Towers **76**
   Will Rogers State Historic Park **87**
Gus's Barbecue **32**
H.M.S. Bounty **48**
HAL BLAINE
   Pink's Hot Dogs **51**
HAPPY HOUR
   El Coyote Café **36**
   Smoke House, The **56**
HARRY HARRISON
   Chips Restaurant **68**
HARRY OLIVER
   Tam O'Shanter **27**
Harvey's Broiler (Bob's Big Boy) **74**
Hat, The **64**
HEART ATTACK
   Greenblatt's Famous Deli **78**
Heritage Square **24**
HEROIN
   Pioneer Chicken **20**
HERSHEY BAR
   Greenblatt's Famous Deli **78**
HIKE
   Griffith Park Observatory **24**
   Wattles Park **44**
   Will Rogers State Historic Park **87**
HISTORIC HOUSES
   Alvarado Terrace **46**
   Carroll Avenue **22**
   Clarke Estate **72**
   Dominguez Rancho Adobe **70**
   Heritage Square **24**

HOW TO FIND OLD LOS ANGELES   97

INDEX

Hollyhock House **25**
Lummis House **14**
Will Rogers State Historic Park **87**
Workman and Temple Family Homestead Museum **66**
HOLLENBECK PARK
   Al & Bea's **20**
Hollyhock House **25**
Hollywood Forever Cemetery **38**
HOLLYWOOD FRANKLIN HOTEL
   101 Coffee Shop **36**
Hop Louie **12**
HORSE BARN
   Los Angeles County Arboretum and Botanic Garden **64**
HORSERIDING
   Griffith Park Observatory **24**
   Santa Anita Park **66**
   Will Rogers State Historic Park **87**
HORSESHOE BAR
   Tom Bergin's Public House **52**
Hot 'n Tot **70**
HOT DOG
   Art's Chili Dog Stand **72**
   Canter's Deli **78**
   Carney's **36**
   Original Tommy's Hamburgers **50**
   Pink's Hot Dogs **51**
HOT FUDGE SUNDAE
   Tam O'Shanter **27**
HOT RODS
   Harvey's Broiler (Bob's Big Boy) **74**
HOT SAUCE
   Prince, The **52**
HOTEL
   Biltmore Hotel **8**
   Fountain Coffee Shop at the Beverly Hills Hotel **83**
HOWARD JOHNSON
   Rod's Grill **65**

HUELL HOWSER
   Tally Rand **56**
HUMPHREY BOGART
   Formosa Café **37**
Huntington Desert Garden **32**
ICE AGE
   La Brea Tar Pits **49**
ICE CREAM
   Bob Baker Marionette Theater **46**
   Fosselman's **62**
   Idle Hour, The **54**
INVASION OF THE BODY SNATCHERS
   Mary's Market & Canyon Café **64**
IRISH COFFEE
   Tom Bergin's Public House **52**
ITALIAN FOOD
   Dan Tana's **78**
   Miceli's **41**
JACK SHELDON
   Miceli's **41**
JACK WEBB
   H.M.S. Bounty **48**
JAMES DEAN
   Griffith Park Observatory **24**
JAPANESE FOOD
   Otomisan **20**
JAZZ
   Biltmore Hotel **8**
JESSE LASKY
   Lasky-DeMille Barn **41**
JEWISH FOOD
   Beverlywood Bakery **80**
   Canter's Deli **78**
   Greenblatt's Famous Deli **78**
   Langer's Deli **49**
JIM ROCKFORD
   Chowder Barge **68**
JOHN FANTE
   Los Angeles Public Library **14**
JOHN HUSTON
   Hollywood Forever Cemetery **38**

Jongewaard's Bake n Broil **70**
JUALITA
   Wattles Park **44**
Judson Studios **26**
JULIA BRACKEN WENDT
   Natural History Museum & Exposition Park Rose Garden **49**
KARAOKE
   Venice Room, The **66**
KEYSTONE KOPS
   Original Pantry Café **17**
KIDNAP
   Sister Aimee's Parsonage **27**
KING TUT
   Grauman's Egyptian Theatre **38**
   Vista Theatre **28**
KOREAN FOOD
   Prince, The **52**
Kramer's Pipe & Tobacco Shop **84**
La Brea Tar Pits **49**
La Golondrina Mexican Café **12**
LA STORY
   Gilmore Gas (Starbucks Coffee Shop) **37**
LAKE
   Self-Realization Fellowship Lake Shrine Temple **86**
Langer's Deli **49**
Lanza Brothers Market **12**
Larry Edmunds Bookshop **38**
Lasky-DeMille Barn **41**
LAWRENCE FRANK
   Tam O'Shanter **27**
LAWRENCE TIERNEY
   Boardner's Bar **36**
Lawry's The Prime Rib **84**
LAX AIRPORT
   Dinah's **83**
   Pann's Coffee Shop **84**
   Randy's Donuts **84**
LEG ROOM

INDEX

Vista Theatre **28**
LENNY BRUCE
  Canter's Deli **78**
LIBRARY
  Brand Library & Art Center **30**
  Los Angeles Public Library **14**
LILY POND
  Workman and Temple Family Homestead Museum **66**
LIQUOR STORE
  Lanza Brothers Market **12**
LIVE MUSIC
  Miceli's **41**
LOCOMOTIVES
  Travel Town **28**
LOG CABIN
  Chris & Pitts **72**
Los Angeles City Hall **14**
Los Angeles County Arboretum and Botanic Garden **64**
Los Angeles Public Library **14**
"LUCKY" BALDWIN
  Los Angeles County Arboretum and Botanic Garden **64**
  Santa Anita Park **66**
Lummis House **14**
Macy's (formerly Bullock's Department Store) **34**
MAD MEN
  Rod's Grill **65**
MAGEE'S KITCHEN
  Original Farmer's Market, The **37**
Magic Castle, The **41**
MAGIC & MAGICIANS
  Magic Castle, The **41**
MAJOR LEAGUE BASEBALL
  Jongewaard's Bake n Broil **70**
MANSON FAMILY
  El Coyote Café **36**
Manuel's Original El Tepeyac Café **20**
MARGARITAS
  El Cholo **48**

El Coyote Café **36**
MARILYN MONROE
  Formosa Café **37**
MARKET
  Eastside Market & Italian Deli **11**
  Original Farmer's Market, The **37**
  Grand Central Market **11**
  Lanza Brothers Market **12**
  Mary's Market & Canyon Café **64**
  Papa Cristo's **51**
  Ye Olde King's Head **88**
MARTINIS
  Musso & Frank Grill **41**
Mary's Market & Canyon Café **64**
MASTODON
  La Brea Tar Pits **49**
McDonald's **74**
MEDITERRANEAN
  Huntington Desert Garden **32**
MEMORABILIA
  Derby Restaurant, The **60**
  Galley, The **83**
  Larry Edmunds Bookshop **38**
MEXICAN FOOD
  Al & Bea's **20**
  Chips Restaurant **68**
  El Cholo **48**
  El Coyote Café **36**
  La Golondrina Mexican Café **12**
  Rod's Grill **65**
  Tito's Tacos **87**
Miceli's **41**
MICKEY COHEN
  Boardner's Bar **36**
MID-CENTURY MENU
  Clearman's Steak 'n Stein **58**
MIDNIGHT AT PINK'S
  Pink's Hot Dogs **51**
MILK

Broguiere's Farm Fresh Dairy **58**
MINIATURE RAILWAY
  Travel Town **28**
MINT TEA
  Moun of Tunis **41**
MISSOURI
  Bear Pit Bar-B-Q, The **54**
MODERNISM
  Clarke Estate **72**
MONASTERY
  Vedanta Society of Southern California **44**
MONK
  Vedanta Society of Southern California **44**
MOONCAKES
  Phoenix Bakery **17**
MOSAIC FLOOR
  Grandma Prisbrey's Bottle Village **54**
Moun of Tunis **41**
MURALS
  Embers Lounge, The **62**
  Biltmore Hotel **8**
  Los Angeles Public Library **14**
MUSEUM
  Dominguez Rancho Adobe **70**
  La Brea Tar Pits **49**
  Lasky-DeMille Barn **41**
  Natural History Museum & Exposition Park Rose Garden **49**
  Sister Aimee's Parsonage **27**
  Travel Town **28**
  Workman and Temple Family Homestead Museum **66**
MUSIC
  La Golondrina Mexican Café **12**
MUSICAL PRODUCTIONS
  Bob Baker Marionette Theater **46**
MUSICIANS

HOW TO FIND OLD LOS ANGELES   99

INDEX

Greenblatt's Famous Deli **78**
Musso & Frank Grill **41**
MUSTARD
   Philippe The Original **17**
MUTINY ON THE BOUNTY
   Chowder Barge **68**
   Galley, The **83**
Natural History Museum & Exposition Park Rose Garden **49**
NATURE
   Confluence of the L.A. River and Arroyo Seco **11**
   Serra Springs **87**
NEW MEXICO
   Lummis House **14**
Nick's Coffee Shop **50**
NORA EPHRON
   Langer's Deli **49**
Norms La Cienega **41**
OBSERVATION DECK
   Los Angeles City Hall **14**
OBSERVATORY
   Griffith Park Observatory **24**
Oceanic Arts **65**
OCTAGONAL HOUSE
   Heritage Square **24**
ONION RINGS
   Clearman's Steak 'n Stein **58**
ORCHARD
   Wattles Park **44**
Original Pantry Café **17**
OSCAR WENDEROTH
   Pasadena US Post Office **34**
Otomisan **20**
Pacific Dining Car **50**
PALEONTOLOGISTS
   La Brea Tar Pits **49**
PANCAKES
   Dinah's **83**
   Tal's Cafe **76**
Pann's Coffee Shop **84**
Papa Cristo's **51**
PARK
   Brand Library & Art Center **30**

Griffith Park Observatory **24**
Wattles Park **44**
Will Rogers State Historic Park **87**
Workman and Temple Family Homestead Museum **66**
PARTY ROOM
   Bob Baker Marionette Theater **46**
Pasadena US Post Office **34**
PASTRAMI
   Greenblatt's Famous Deli **78**
   Hat, The **64**
   Langer's Deli **49**
PATIO
   La Golondrina Mexican Café **12**
PATTY MELT
   Nick's Coffee Shop **50**
PENCIL COLLECTION
   Grandma Prisbrey's Bottle Village **54**
PEOPLE-WATCHING
   Astro Family Restaurant **22**
   La Golondrina Mexican Café **12**
PERSIAN CARPETS
   Moun of Tunis **41**
PETER LORRE
   Hollywood Forever Cemetery **38**
PHARMACY
   Fair Oaks Pharmacy and Soda Fountain **30**
PHIL SPECTOR
   Canter's Deli **78**
Philippe The Original **17**
Phoenix Bakery **17**
PICNIC
   Dominguez Rancho Adobe **70**
   Hollywood Forever Cemetery **38**
   Will Rogers State Historic Park **87**

Pie 'n Burger **34**
PIER
   Santa Monica Pier Carousel **86**
   Tony's on the Pier **70**
PIES
   Apple Pan, The **80**
   House of Pies **25**
   Jongewaard's Bake n Broil **70**
   Pie 'n Burger **34**
   STOX Restaurant & Bakery **76**
Pink's Hot Dogs **51**
Pioneer Chicken **20**
PIPES
   Kramer's Pipe & Tobacco Shop **84**
PIZZA
   Casa Bianca **30**
   Miceli's **41**
   Patsy Pizza **37**
Plaza, The **18**
POLYNESIAN
   Oceanic Arts **65**
   Tiki-Ti **28**
POOL TABLES
   Gage Bowl **73**
POST OFFICE
   Pasadena US Post Office **34**
POUTINE
   Arsenal, The **80**
Prince, The **52**
PRIVATE CLUB
   Magic Castle, The **41**
PRIVATE PARTIES
   Cicada Club Restaurant **10**
   Taylor's Steakhouse **52**
PROPS
   Oceanic Arts **65**
PUB
   Red Lion Tavern **27**
   Tom Bergin's Public House **52**
   Ye Olde King's Head **88**
QUEEN ANNE MANSION
   Los Angeles County Arboretum

INDEX

and Botanic Garden **64**
RACETRACK
   Santa Anita Park **66**
RAILS
   Angel's Flight Railway
   Carney's **36**
   Pacific Dining Car **50**
   Travel Town **28**
   Union Station **18**
RAMAKRISHNA ORDER
   Vedanta Society of Southern California **44**
Randy's Donuts **84**
RAT PACK
   Chez Jay's **80**
RAY BRADBURY
   Los Angeles Public Library **14**
RAYMOND CHANDLER
   Galley, The **83**
   Musso & Frank Grill **41**
REBEL WITHOUT A CAUSE
   Griffith Park Observatory **24**
RECYCLING
   Watts Towers **76**
Red Lion Tavern **27**
Reel Inn **86**
REPLICA DRUGSTORE
   Heritage Square **24**
RESTROOMS
   Grauman's Chinese Theatre **38**
RICHARD NEUTRA
   Red Lion Tavern **27**
RIVER
   Confluence of the L.A. River and Arroyo Seco **11**
Rod's Grill **65**
RODNEY KING
   Art's Chili Dog Stand **72**
ROLLER SKATING
   Harvey's Broiler (Bob's Big Boy) **74**
ROLLIN B. LANE MANSION
   Magic Castle, The **41**
ROMAN COURTYARD
   Clarke Estate **72**
ROSE GARDEN
   Natural History Museum & Exposition Park Rose Garden **49**
ROSE WATER
   Moun of Tunis **41**
ROUTE 66
   Barney's Beanery **78**
   Fair Oaks Pharmacy and Soda Fountain **30**
   Rod's Grill **65**
RUDOLPH VALENTINO
   Hollywood Forever Cemetery **38**
RUNYON CANYON
   Wattles Park **44**
RYE BREAD
   Beverlywood Bakery **80**
   Langer's Deli **49**
SABER-TOOTHED CAT
   La Brea Tar Pits **49**
SALVATION ARMY THRIFT SHOP
   Alvarado Terrace **46**
San Antonio Winery **18**
Santa Anita Park **66**
Santa Monica Pier Carousel **86**
SAUSAGE
   Red Lion Tavern **27**
SAWDUST
   Bear Pit Bar-B-Q, The **54**
   Philippe The Original **17**
SCHWARTZ'S
   Langer's Deli **49**
SCOTTISH RESTAURANT
   Tam O'Shanter **27**
SEAFOOD
   Reel Inn **86**
   Smoke House, The **56**
   Tony's on the Pier **70**
SEAGULLS
   Tony's on the Pier **70**
Self-Realization Fellowship Lake Shrine Temple **86**

Serra Springs **87**
SHACK
   Reel Inn **86**
SHARON TATE
   El Coyote Café **36**
SHOESHINE
   Union Station **18**
SHRINE
   Self-Realization Fellowship Lake Shrine Temple **86**
SIMON RODIA
   Watts Towers **76**
Sister Aimee's Parsonage **27**
SLEIGHT OF HAND
   Magic Castle, The **41**
SMOKING
   Kramer's Pipe & Tobacco Shop **84**
   Tiki-Ti **28**
SNACK BAR
   Vista Theatre **28**
SOCKS
   Macy's (formerly Bullock's Department Store) **34**
SODA FOUNTAIN
   Fair Oaks Pharmacy and Soda Fountain **30**
SOURDOUGH
   Original Pantry Café **17**
SPANISH FOOD
   El Cid **22**
SPEAKEASY
   Arsenal, The **80**
SPORTS BAR
   Gus's Barbecue **32**
SPRING
   Self-Realization Fellowship Lake Shrine Temple **86**
   Serra Springs **87**
SQUAW MAN, THE
   Lasky-DeMille Barn **41**
ST PATRICK'S DAY
   Tom Bergin's Public House **52**
ST. SOPHIA CATHEDRAL

INDEX

Papa Cristo's **51**
STARBUCKS
  Gilmore Gas (Starbucks Coffee Shop) **37**
STEAK
  Arsenal, The **80**
  Clearman's Steak 'n Stein **58**
  Dal Rae, The **60**
  Lawry's The Prime Rib **84**
  Pacific Dining Car **50**
  Taylor's Steakhouse **52**
  Venice Room, The **66**
STEAK SAUCE
  Pacific Dining Car **50**
STOX Restaurant & Bakery **76**
STREETCARS
  Travel Town **28**
STRIP JOINT
  Arsenal, The **80**
SUBURB
  Carroll Avenue **22**
SUNSET STRIP
  Carney's **36**
SURF N TURF
  Chez Jay's **80**
  Taylor's Steakhouse **52**
SWAMI PRABHAVANANDA
  Vedanta Society of Southern California **44**
SWANS
  Self-Realization Fellowship Lake Shrine Temple **86**
SWEET POTATO FRIES
  Carney's **36**
SWINGERS
  Dresden Room **22**
TACOS
  Grand Central Market **11**
  Tito's Tacos **87**
TAIL-OF-THE-PUP
  Pink's Hot Dogs **51**
Taix **27**
TAJ MAHAL
  Vedanta Society of Southern California **44**
Tal's Cafe **76**
Tally Rand **56**
Tam O'Shanter **27**
TAMALES
  El Cholo **48**
TASTING ROOM
  San Antonio Winery **18**
TAVERNA
  Papa Cristo's **51**
TAXIDERMY
  Natural History Museum & Exposition Park Rose Garden **49**
Taylor's Steakhouse **52**
TEA ROOM
  Ye Olde King's Head **88**
TEMPLE
  Brand Library & Art Center **30**
  Self-Realization Fellowship Lake Shrine Temple **86**
  Vedanta Society of Southern California **44**
  Workman and Temple Family Homestead Museum **66**
THEATRE
  Bob Baker Marionette Theater **46**
  Broadway Theater District **8**
  Clearman's Steak 'n Stein **58**
  Grauman's Chinese Theatre **38**
  Grauman's Egyptian Theatre **38**
  Vista Theatre **28**
TIKI
  Oceanic Arts **65**
  Tiki-Ti **28**
Tiki-Ti **28**
TIME CAPSULE
  Tal's Cafe **76**
  Otomisan **20**
Tito's Tacos **87**
TOBACCO
  Kramer's Pipe & Tobacco Shop **84**
Tom Bergin's Public House **52**
Tony's on the Pier **70**
TRAIN STATION
  Union Station **18**
Travel Town **28**
TUNISIAN FOOD
  Moun of Tunis **41**
TURKEY SANDWICH
  Tally Rand **56**
TURTLES
  Self-Realization Fellowship Lake Shrine Temple **86**
Union Station **18**
Vedanta Society of Southern California **44**
Venice Room, The **66**
VICTORIAN
  Carroll Avenue **22**
  Heritage Square **24**
  Los Angeles County Arboretum and Botanic Garden **64**
VIEW
  Brand Library & Art Center **30**
  Hollyhock House **25**
  Los Angeles City Hall **14**
  Santa Anita Park **66**
  Tony's on the Pier **70**
VILLAGE
  Plaza, The **18**
VINTAGE PHOTOGRAPHS
  Fosselman's **62**
  Mary's Market & Canyon Café **64**
  Venice Room, The **66**
VINTNERS
  San Antonio Winery **18**
VIRGIN MARY
  Manuel's Original El Tepeyac Café **20**
Vista Theatre **28**
WALK
  Carroll Avenue **22**
  Confluence of the L.A. River

INDEX

and Arroyo Seco **11**
Los Angeles County Arboretum and Botanic Garden **64**
Wattles Park **44**
Workman and Temple Family Homestead Museum **66**
WALT DISNEY
  Tam O'Shanter **27**
WALTER VAN DE KAMP
  Tam O'Shanter **27**
WALTER WINCHELL
  H.M.S. Bounty **48**
WARNER BROTHERS STUDIO
  Smoke House, The **56**
WARREN ZEVON
  Pioneer Chicken **20**
Wattles Park **44**a
Watts Towers **76**
WEDDING VENUE
  Clarke Estate **72**
  Wattles Park **44**
Will Rogers State Historic Park **87**
WILLIAM LEES JUDSON
  Judson Studios **26**
WILLLIAM FAULKNER
  Musso & Frank Grill **41**
WINDMILL
  Self-Realization Fellowship Lake Shrine Temple **86**
WINDSOR APARTMENT COMPLEX
  Prince, The **52**
WINE
  Pacific Dining Car **50**
  Pie 'n Burger **34**
WINERY
  San Antonio Winery **18**
WINSTON CHURCHILL
  H.M.S. Bounty **48**
Workman and Temple Family Homestead Museum **66**
WORLD'S FAIR
  Brand Library & Art Center **30**
WRECKING CREW

Pink's Hot Dogs **51**
Ye Olde King's Head **88**
YOGA
  Self-Realization Fellowship Lake Shrine Temple **86**